COOKING ON WHEELS

COOKING ON WHEELS

A cookbook for travel trailers,
pick-up campers, tent campers,
motor homes, and all recreational
vehicles with cooking facilities

by
Arlene Strom

with a Foreword by Helen Byam Schwamborn

Illustrations by Roger W. Palmquist

The Bond Wheelwright Company, Freeport, Maine

Published by The Bond Wheelwright Company
Freeport, Maine 04032

Library of Congress Catalog Card #: 73-112688
SBN # 87027-111-3
Manufactured in the United States of America

First Printing: April 1970
Second Printing: January 1971

*To Ken and Bob
who have been my tasters,
my proofreaders
and always my inspiration to cook*

FOREWORD

While traveling by trailer, chalking up more than 100,000 miles, Mrs. Strom compiled an exciting collection of recipes adapted to travel trailer cooking. To inspire you to try your hand at this lively game of trailer cooking, she shares with you her recipes, suggestions, and tid-bits of helpful information in COOKING ON WHEELS.

Her book is a stimulus for the cook on wheels. She invites you to explore the world of enjoyable and free-wheeling cooking. She challenges you to expose new layers of talent by solving menus in a most creative way.

Through reading COOKING ON WHEELS you will capture the intriguing and ever changing facets of cooking on wheels. It is a sensible approach to cooking which makes the book a practical one for both the epicure and neophyte. The recipes are popular ones, many are old favorites, and all have been tried and proven.

The author skillfully leads her readers from a gastronomic splurge to a "quickie" meal. She believes in shortcuts and appreciates their importance, as she does the start-from-scratch cuisine for more auspicious occasions. She believes in giving recipes a personal touch.

When she first began to trailer, Mrs. Strom said that she had to carry ideas and recipes on cards. Trailer cookbooks didn't exist to meet her needs, and there wasn't room in the trailer (along with the family, her husband and son) for all the books she valued for ideas and recipes. She wondered if other trailerists didn't share her dilemma. She decided that they did, and that she would incorporate into a single volume, tailored expressly for the trailer cook, the mass of data she had accumulated through the years.

Mrs. Strom enjoys having guests and giving dinner parties in her trailer. She enjoys baking, which she says includes everything — even Swedish rye bread. She confides that the ideas and recipes in her book are mostly gifts of family and friends, many from the Swedish tradition of cooking.

Mrs. Strom features recipes, hints, ideas and the employment of methods conducive to efficient operation in the trailer. Trailer travel gets one away from the daily grind of shopping in the same markets, away from preparing and serving meals in the same setting, and away from always adhering to the conventions of established home-town customs.

A seasoned trailerist, Mrs. Strom stocks only a few days' supply and indulges in the pleasure of shopping along the way when traveling. Stopping at local markets can be crowned with adventure. One may stop at a general store where groceries are shelved along with tools, household generals, and clothing; one may seek the grandeur of supermarkets, or the ritziest gourmet shops.

Schedules are flexible — day's end might be beside a lily-mantled lake, or on the measureless open desert. Dinner may be savored in the glow of a crimson sun setting behind purple hills, or beside the pounding surf or a quiet stream.

Even the table can be a vision of one's ingenuity . . . in fact the imagination of the entire family can be unleashed in the clever fabrication of fanciful decorations made of weeds, wild flowers, pods, driftwood, pine cones, sea shells or whatever is at hand.

COOKING ON WHEELS takes a different approach than the usual cook book: Top of the Stove Cookery; Using Your Oven; Recipes with Little or No Preparation; Organizing the Trailer Kitchen; Equipment; Food Purchasing and Storage; and Helpful Hints.

FOREWORD

This is a comprehensive how-to cook book for trailering, with jotting space allowed for personal additions. It is the substance of firsthand knowledge of cooking on wheels, and it will be a valuable addition to one's trailer library.

The Stroms have been trailering since 1961, when they purchased their first travel trailer. Mr. Strom is a Chaplain in the Veterans Administration Hospital system. As Deputy Director of VA Chaplains, he is required to travel a great deal. In the summer the Stroms hook up their Airstream and accompany Mr. Strom to wherever his duties may take him. One summer they traveled from their home in Maryland to the Rockies, to Nova Scotia, and back to Maryland. Summer for the Strom family is synonymous with joyous adventure.

HELEN BYAM SCHWAMBORN

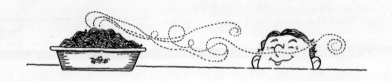

ACKNOWLEDGMENTS

No cook is completely original. We have all learned from someone else, and most of us began our education in our mother's kitchen. From there our education broadened to the kitchens of our friends, and the wonderful world of cook books. To all, from Mother on down, I owe a debt of gratitude which I can best try to repay by sharing their ideas with others. Where possible I have identified the sources of my recipes.

A word of thanks is due Helen Byam Schwamborn and Lorraine Peterson, fellow trailerites, for their encouragement in producing this book. To my friends the Dr. Robert Bowdens for introducing our family to the wonderful world of trailering; to artist Roger Palmquist and photographer Hank Dollard; and to my publisher Thea Wheelwright whose skills and insights have been so very helpful, my special thanks.

I would also like to thank my fellow trailer cooks, and especially those of the Mid-Atlantic Unit of the Wally Byam Caravan Club International for the many sharing experiences in Belle Sessions and around delightful potluck tables.

No word of appreciation would be complete without mention of my husband and son who have tasted every recipe, helped in production, read proof, and accepted my busyness over a two-year period.

To all, my sincere thanks!

ARLENE STROM

xi

CONTENTS

*(Note: Blank pages are provided at the ends of Chapters III, IV,
and V for recording your own favorite recipes.)*

INTRODUCTION

This book is designed to help your "fun" dreams of trailer living come true. Keeping house in a trailer *can* be fun! This is especially true of your cooking.

We purchased our first trailer — a 16 foot Airstream — in 1961. Almost immediately my husband was transferred and we set out for our new location, towing our "home" behind us. As it turned out, my husband and I, with our eight-year-old son, were to live in our new vacation trailer for almost two months. My first inclination was to think of cooking in the same terms as I had in the modern and well-equipped kitchen I had just left. Since my trailer was new and modern it should have worked fine. But there really is a difference. Instead of a dozen cupboards . . . . . well, you can about guess what a 16-footer will hold. Every time I planned for something, it seemed I was missing that special pan, that electrical gadget, or the not-too-often-used ingredient.

The difference in trailer cooking grew on me, especially when we began to take trips. I would try to plan food that would be quick and simple to prepare. Long hours in meal preparation would keep me from enjoying the vacation fun of family and friends. When we left for a trip I would stuff recipes in my purse. There didn't seem to be enough space for numerous cook books, but without my "handbag specials," I would always be wondering if I had forgotten an ingredient, or if my oven temperature was correct.

Three trailers and more than a hundred thousand miles of trailering later, many of my original recipes are still in use. Through the gracious friendships known so well to the "trailering set," dozens of new recipes have been added. We've added more cupboards, a good oven, a small freezing compartment in the refrigerator, and this all helps, but the basic practices are the same. Preparing breakfasts, lunches, dinners or snacks can be a pleasure if you plan well.

My trailer friends have encouraged this publication, but it should be of interest to the thousands of women who never have the fun of cooking on wheels. Trailer cooking and cooking in a well-equipped home kitchen often have the same goal — quick and simple food preparation with a minimum of work. I have emphasized the relatively simple and easy-to-prepare dishes, but have also included recipes for trailer cooks who in the cool of their air-conditioned trailers entertain guests and spend months in one locale or another. Also included are some ideas for stocking a trailer kitchen and for the equipment that I feel makes for good cooking. To someone who is just starting out on the exciting road of trailering, the latter can be very helpful in avoiding needless expense. Since pot-luck suppers are so much a part of trailering, especially with the many existing trailer clubs, many recipes of this type have been included.

This is not a book of "menu planning." Most families develop definite eating habits, and may not like the same combination of foods. If one is looking for something new and easy to try, one would not necessarily set out to try an entirely new menu for any one meal. Furthermore, the situation will determine the type of dish one is searching for. Your trailer might be parked in some isolated spot where the entire family is enjoying recreation and the wonders of nature and you are miles from the supermarket. In such a spot, you might not be hooked up to electricity, so any appliances you might have with you could not be put into use. But searching through the chapters on "Top of the Stove Cookery," "Using Your Oven," or "Little or No Preparation," you are sure to find some rather simple recipe calling for canned, frozen or dried ingredients that will provide the makings of a casserole dish or some delightful dessert for your family.

The trailer kitchen is not too unlike the kitchen of the working girl or the bride. Usually equipment is at a minimum, and time is often a factor which would prevent the preparation of more elaborate foods. This book will be a source of help in just such a situation.

What is said in this book about travel trailer cooking applies as well to all types of recreational vehicles that have cooking facilities "on wheels" — could also be used in the boat galley!

I.

MEAL PLANNING AND PURCHASING OF FOOD

These two items go naturally together. The purchase of food is always dependent upon the shopping possibilities along the route, the equipment carried, the length of the trip, the amount of storage available, the number of people traveling, and — says my husband — the money available. Let's talk a little about all of these things — except the money.

Most meals on short vacations should be simple. After a long day's drive, you are generally not in the mood to try an elaborate dish. If the family is out seeing the sights, the thought of working up a fancy dinner has little appeal. But in spite of it all, most families agree that part of the fun of vacationing is enjoying good food.

SOME BASIC ORGANIZATION

To a person with a new trailer, the thought of planning meals is sometimes frightening. It need not be. Before you do anything else, do some organizing. A Master Check List is a must! Before every trip, run down the list to make sure each item is in the trailer. Part of this list will include the things you consider essential for the smooth operation of your trailer kitchen. Just as one pair of shoes cannot fit each child in your family, so one list of equipment cannot fit exactly each family that is trailering or camping. If you are a family that enjoys a few of the luxuries that remind you of home, you will perhaps include some of these things in your packing. If your group is large and your space extremely limited, you will weigh the value of each item before deciding that it is an absolute essential. But any list that you make must start somewhere, and our list on page 131 is that "somewhere." Add to it, subtract from it, but do develop your own check list in order that the things really necessary for a good trip are not left at home. It takes but a minute while your husband is hitching up to go down the list and assure yourself that no important item is missing. As you trailer or camp year after year, you will quite automatically acquire items which can become standard equipment in your trailer and never need be taken out of it. This will probably be true of bedding, kitchen pots and pans, and perhaps some personal gear such as toothbrushes for the family, etc. The less that has to be carried into your home from the trailer when you return, the more you will enjoy that quick weekend trip, or for that matter, any trip!

Keep in mind the limitations of your kitchen. If there are items you cannot leave permanently in your trailer, be sure they are on the Master Check List. How free of KP chores do you want to be? Choose recipes and foods that your family likes, but coordinate their likes with your built-in limitations, the time required to prepare them, the labor involved in making the meal, and the cleanup. Be constantly on the alert for new recipes and different ways of doing things in your particular situation. Especially on the road, attractive meals are quite acceptably served on plastic or paper plates. We use them constantly. The plastic cups that have a paper insert are excellent for warm beverages, soups, chili, etc.

SPACE IS LIMITED! It follows that outfitting and equipping your trailer kitchen is always a matter of deciding how important each item is to your cooking. How you load the trailer is also very important if it is to tow properly. The kitchen must not be weighed down with improperly placed heavy equipment. Any heavy object should be placed as low as possible in the trailer, and preferably over or near the wheels. Do not place heavy objects in the upper compartments of your cabinets. A good grade of plastics is preferable over metal — both because of the weight and because plastic does not leave black marks on shelves. Place a layer of very thin foam rubber on your shelves. This will help to keep things in place when the trailer is in motion, and will keep metal objects from rubbing and marking the bottom. No foam? Try a bath towel.

POTS AND PANS. If your trailer does not have an oven, a folding one of stainless steel is a wonderful addition. These fold away when not in use. Having an oven will increase the number of things you can include in the menu. Among your pots and pans, a good skillet with a tight-fitting cover is a must. Since there will be days when the weather is hot and you will not want to have the oven heating the trailer, many things can be prepared on top of the stove. If the skillet is one with a Teflon interior, much of the mess of cleanup can be eliminated. Simply wipe out the inside with a paper towel when you have finished using it, then a quick whisk with soap suds and the pan is ready to be tucked away again. Of equal importance to me is a good double boiler. When not in use as a double boiler, you have two separate pans. The insert pan can also be used as a bowl for mixing, or for salads. If you have no oven, you can heat rolls in the top of your double boiler. In selecting pans, use pans that will "nest." It saves space. If you are short of burners when cooking, and you have one pan in which food has already been heated, turn the cover over on the pan still "working" and place the already heated pan on the over-turned cover to keep food warm. If you are lucky enough to have a set of pans just for your trailer, select them with these things in mind.

A CASSEROLE is an important item, as so many trailerites are great "potluckers." Select one that will withstand traveling and yet be attractive. Many of the new colored Teflon lined Dutch ovens can double as casseroles. A casserole need not be glass. If it is, cushion it while you travel by wrapping it in a bath towel and storing it in your oven or any other available space.

SERVING DISHES may be kept to a minimum and storage space saved if food is served directly out of the pan or utensil in which it has been prepared. You'll not mind this if you select pots and pans with an eye to beauty, and in keeping with the color scheme of the rest of your trailer kitchen and equipment. A good nest of bowls with covers can help in the serving of food, as well as in the preparation of food, and the covers can assure storage in the refrigerator.

STORAGE is on a smaller scale than in your home, so buy in smaller quantities when marketing. Store the canned goods low in the trailer, preferably over the axle. Potato chips, crackers, cookies, and all of your paper goods ride very nicely in upper compartments.

WATER is in limited supply — unless your trailer is connected to a water line — so its conservation is of utmost importance in food preparation and cleanup. At home I find myself rinsing utensils under the hot water faucet as I go through meal preparation. In the trailer, wiping them with a paper towel right after use will save work and water in the later washing process. There are a number of ways one can cut down on the volume of soiled plates and bowls when water is limited. Using one-pot meals is one good way. Maybe some day our trailer manufacturers will be making trailer dishwashers with a reusable water supply.

PACKING EQUIPMENT AND SUPPLIES is a skill in which you will constantly improve. Whether it be the shelves of the refrigerator or the shelves in your cabinets, never travel with articles loosely packed. One tightly packed shelf is better than two shelves where loosely standing objects can roll around or be bumped, creating spilling problems. In our first trailer I had a problem with eggs breaking in the refrigerator. Sometimes in desperation before leaving home on weekend trips when I knew I would use eggs for scrambling, I would break them into a plastic bowl that had a tight cover, and store them in the refrigerator until needed. One day I decided a bath towel on the shelf on my refrigerator might help. After that — no more broken eggs.

Many unbreakable containers will simplify housekeeping — plastic boxes, bags, bottles. One box can hold many small items, thus preventing them from rolling around. This is true in any part of your trailer, from drug items in the bathroom to games, pencils, papers, maps, etc.

MEALS AND MENUS

For weekend trips a quick planning of the menus for each meal will save time and money in shopping. List all the things you need to purchase before departure. For a longer trip, make some general plans for several breakfasts, dinners and lunches, anticipating that there will be opportunity for shopping en route. In summer it is often pleasant to shop for seasonal foods at the roadside stands. Nowadays almost every town has a modern supermarket. Their parking lots are large enough in most cases so that you can pull in and park off to the side without obstructing traffic. If, however, you are planning a trip into a "wilderness" area, your planning must be more specific.

Carry some of the new freeze-dried foods that are sold through camping supply stores, trailer dealers, etc. They are light in weight, do not require refrigeration, and will keep almost indefinitely. All that is required is the addition of liquid in the preparation of these dehydrated foods. There are some very attractive items, including main dishes, available in this form. Catalogs from several firms specializing in these foods are available upon request. Listed below are several of the firms:

Alpine Hut, Inc.
4725 30th Ave. NE
Seattle, Washington 98105

Canoe Country Outfitter, Inc.
629 E. Sheridan St.
Ely, Minnesota 55731

L. L. Bean, Inc.
Freeport, Maine 04032

Remington's
11230 Georgia Ave.
Wheaton, Maryland 20902

Chuck Wagon Foods
176 Oak Street
Newton, Massachusetts 02164

Rich-Moor Corp.
616 N. Robertson Blvd.
Los Angeles, California 90069

Hoigaards, Inc.
3550 S. Highway 100
Minneapolis, Minnesota 55416

Skimeister Ski Shop
Main Street
North Woodstock, N.H. 03262

Laake and Joys Co.
1433 N. Water Street
Milwaukee, Wisconsin 53202

S. S. Pierce
133 Brookline Avenue
Boston, Massachusetts 02117

Perma-Pak
40 E. 2430 South (Robert Ave.)
Salt Lake City, Utah 84115

Wilderness House
1310 Commonwealth Ave.
Boston, Massachusetts 02134

Wally Byam Stores
(at your nearest Airstream Trailer Dealer)

QUICK START IN THE MORNING. When we are travel-
ing and are anxious to get on the road in the morning, we fix what
we call our "breakfast on the run." It is quick and easy. I serve
dry cereal in the individual cartons, slitting along the cutting lines
and using each box as its own bowl.

On a cold day when you want something hot, an instant warm
cereal is available. It is made by pouring the contents of a packet
into a bowl and simply adding boiling water. Orange juice is
served in paper cups. A quick cup of instant coffee is served with
a sweet roll or doughnut. With just spoons to rinse, we are on our
way in no time at all. Should you feel that you want to perk a
pot of coffee, make a large pot, pouring what you don't use for

breakfast into a thermos to have in the car as you travel. Of course, instant coffee can be carried in the same way.

COOKING AT HIGH ALTITUDES. If you are up where the air is clear and the sky blue (maybe you can tell we are "Wyomingites" at heart), remember that foods cooked in water take longer to cook, the higher up you go. It takes about twice as long to cook food a mile up (in a place like Denver) than it does at sea level. This, of course, is due to the fact that the boiling point of water drops two degrees for every thousand feet of altitude. (We learned the hard way when we first lived in the area of the Rockies.) Baking does not require much more time, but allow extra time for the cooking of any food that depends upon the boiling point of water. If you forget, you may be eating later than you think. Following are adjustments for cake baking which must be made at high altitude:

If you are using all-purpose flour or cake flour at 5,000 feet altitude, add 2 more tablespoons of flour per cup. If the recipe calls for baking powder, baking soda, or both, make changes according to the table below:

Sea Level	5,000 feet
1 teaspoon	½ teaspoon more
1½ teaspoons	¾ teaspoon more
2 teaspoons	1¼ teaspoons more
2½ teaspoons	1½ teaspoons more
3 teaspoons	1½ teaspoons more
3½ teaspoons	2 teaspoons more
4 teaspoons	2 teaspoons more

II.

HELPFUL HINTS

Many of the little things that are done in our homes to save time and cleanup of equipment are also good hints for the trailer. But living in a trailer is a little different. One is anxious to have as little as possible to do in order to enjoy people, the world around us, the wonders of nature, etc., hence every little trick that can save seconds becomes a part of trailer life. It is in this light that this chapter on "Helpful Hints" is presented. I'm sure that many of my friends who have trailered for years could add endlessly to this list.

For quick reference, key words and phrases are in caps.

FOOD HINTS

To get just a FEW DROPS OF LEMON (or a teaspoon or so of lemon juice), you don't have to cut the fruit. Warm lemon to room temperature (they are much juicier at room temperature), and then jab a fork into the end of the lemon. You can squeeze out as much as you need and store the lemon without having it dry out before you need it again.

When COOKING FROM A NEW RECIPE, look through the recipe first and use your measuring spoons and cups first for the dry ingredients, then for the liquid ingredients. This SAVES WASHING AND DRYING them during the preparation.

You can WARM A CAN OF VEGETABLES to just the right temperature in its can, thus having eliminated some of your "after meal cleanup." Place the can in a pot of cold water and heat only until the water begins to boil. Then slowly open the can, to avoid having the contents spurt out. If you are in a trailer that does not have a water heater, save the pan of hot water for your dishwashing later.

When BARBECUING out of doors, line your grill with foil and put the coals in it. When your cooking is over and the coals have burned out, wrap the foil around the ashes and dispose of the package.

When preparing dinner, save an empty tin can or an empty milk carton in which to DISPOSE OF GARBAGE from your meal. Stand it in the sink or on your drainboard during your preparation of the meal and you will have a place in which to pour grease or dispose of odds and ends which would quickly leak through a paper sack.

As is mentioned further on in a recipe for flank steak, you can successfully MARINATE MEAT FOR YOUR EVENING MEAL while spending the day traveling. In the morning before you start out, test two plastic bags by running a bit of water into them to make sure they are leakproof. Pour out the water and place one bag inside the other. Into this double plastic bag, pour your marinade, place meat inside, and tightly secure top with a "twistie." Place this in your kitchen sink while you spend the day on the road. The motion of the moving trailer will keep the steak well marinated. When you stop for the night, set a few coals out in your portable charcoal burner, and your dinner is well on its way to being prepared.

If you are MELTING CHOCOLATE, line the top of the double boiler with foil and place chocolate in this. When melted, scrape from the foil with a rubber scraper, and dispose of the foil.

If you make ICED TEA and it suddenly clouds up and is no

longer the clear jewel-like beverage you had hoped for, pour just a bit of boiling water into it and it will clear. Did you ever try iced tea and gingerale together? Very good.

If you should find that your WHIPPING CREAM is not whipping, add a teaspoon of lemon juice to it and this should do the trick.

PIMENTOS will keep longer in the refrigerator after being opened if you add just a little vinegar to the jar. The pimentos will not take on the taste of the vinegar.

If your SALAD GREENS have lost their crispness they can be revitalized by the addition of 1 tablespoon of vinegar to some cold water. Soak the greens in this for 15 minutes.

If you are in a hurry to make POTATO SALAD, instead of cooking the potatoes whole, peel and dice the potatoes first, then cook. They will be ready to mix into the salad in a matter of minutes.

If you are making GRAVY from the drippings of a roast and find grease swimming on top of the gravy, pouring in a bit of cream will make the grease disappear like magic.

NUTS stored in the freezer will keep fresh indefinitely. MARSHMALLOWS also can be kept for a long period of time in the freezer.

If you DO A LOT OF BAKING, keep a one or two-cup measuring cup in the flour container. There is no need to wash it every time it is used. Or keep all containers used for measuring dry ingredients in a paper bag. This saves time.

When FREEZING FRUIT CAKE AND FRUIT PIES, do not wrap directly in foil, as the combination of acid in fruits and the high degree of moisture causes the foil to pit. It is best to wrap it first in plastic wrap or wax paper and then in foil.

In FREEZING GROUND BEEF, make a few packages of thin layers, separated by freezer paper or double wax paper. Then when you are in a hurry, it's quicker to thaw several thin layers than one large solid piece of meat.

For QUICK COOKING OF BACON for several persons, put bacon in a single layer on broiling pan in 400 degree oven. Bake 8-10 minutes. There is no need to turn bacon. It remains flat and there is very little shrinkage of meat.

To GREASE A PAN, keep a stick of butter or margarine in the refrigerator. Open one end only, and rub that end around the pan. No greasy fingers!

After using juice from an orange or lemon, put the rind in a plastic bag and freeze it. Then when you need GRATED RIND in a recipe, remove from freezer and grate while still cold. You can also grate rinds first and store in small container in freezer.

When HARD-COOKING EGGS, you can keep them from cracking during cooking by first poking a hole in one end with a pin or large needle.

If you put HARD-COOKED EGGS into the refrigerator to cool, mark them first with a grease pencil to keep them from being mixed with the uncooked eggs.

A GREASE PENCIL is always handy in my kitchen at home as well as in my trailer. It is excellent for marking the contents of plastic containers that are going into refrigerator or freezer. When date or contents mark is no longer needed on a cover, a piece of dry facial tissue rubbed over the marking will quickly remove it.

For an ATTRACTIVE ROUND LOAF of pumpkin, banana, nut, or orange bread, bake in a #1 size can which has been washed clean. Fill 2/3 full. It will require about 40-45 minutes of baking time.

A few helpful hints in PIE BAKING: To prevent soaking of the bottom crust in berry pies, sprinkle the bottom with flour. Also bake quickly. To prevent the soaking of the bottom crust in a custard pie, brush with beaten egg white. Also, use scalding milk, and pour the filling warm into the crust.

When traveling or picnicking, do not FROST CUPCAKES in usual manner. Instead, split cup cakes and place frosting between the two halves.

You may SHORTEN THE BAKING TIME OF A MEAT LOAF by baking in 3-inch muffin pans. Top each one with a square of bacon and bake at 400 degrees for 25 minutes.

If you have a problem with LEAKY MILK CARTONS in your refrigerator due to the carton rubbing on the shelf when the trailer is in motion, place a few sheets of paper toweling under the carton. Do not use cardboard, as this absorbs cooling and will cause your refrigerator to work harder to maintain the proper temperature.

The green discoloration that sometimes appears between the white and the yolk of a HARD-COOKED EGG results from a chemical reaction which is harmless. To help prevent this discoloration, however, cook eggs at low temperatures, avoid overcooking, and cool promptly.

When SLICING REFRIGERATOR COOKIES, use a wire cheese cutter. Slices will be thin and even.

A FOOLPROOF WAY TO UNMOLD GELATIN is to

grease mold generously with cooking oil and chill it in refrigerator first. Blot up any excess oil with a paper towel before pouring gelatin in. Have gelatin fairly well cooled before pouring into mold. Refrigerate in usual manner. Remove mold from refrigerator about 10 minutes before turning gelatin out onto serving plate.

An easy way to UNMOLD GELATIN onto a serving plate with lettuce cupped around it is to place the lettuce on the mold first with the cupped side of the lettuce facing downward over rim of mold. Invert plate on top of lettuce and turn plate and mold over in one motion.

If you want to know the secret of a PERFECTLY SMOOTH AND CLEAR GRAVY OR SAUCE, hunt up Arrowroot and use this as your thickening agent instead of flour or cornstarch. Use 1 tablespoon of arrowroot to 2 tablespoons flour or 1 tablespoon cornstarch. Mix it with water and pour into sauce or gravy. One big advantage is that your gravy will not have a starchy flavor, and best of all, besides giving a perfectly clear, lumpless gravy or sauce, the gravy will not get any thicker if it is reheated or kept warm at serving temperature.

To have perfectly FRESH COFFEE, it should be used within one week of the time the can is opened. If this is not possible, store the can in the refrigerator upside down. (Turning the can upside down will create a vacuum at the top side, thus helping to preserve the freshness of the coffee.)

To FROST CUPCAKES quickly and artistically, hold the cake on the bottom edge, turn upside down and twist lightly into a bowl of fluffy frosting. (No extra utensils to wash!)

It is a good idea when starting a trip to HAVE THE REFRIGERATOR COLD before placing large quantities of food in it. Let it run for several hours before packing. If you are taking foods from your home freezer with you, transfer them to the trailer in their frozen state. They will help to keep your refrigerator cold, and will keep longer than if they have been allowed to thaw first.

If using a GLASS CAKE PAN, always decrease the oven temperature 25 degrees.

GENERAL HINTS

Be very careful what you use for cleaning PLASTIC TRAILER BATHROOM SINKS where the use of scouring powder is not advised. A silver polish such as Wright's Cream does a wonderful cleanup job and will not take the gloss off the plastic.

To remove any MARKS FROM FORMICA COUNTER tops, rub a dampened dishcloth over a bar of soap and rub gently over mark. It disappears like magic.

If you are CLEANING A STAINLESS STEEL SINK, the best cleanser is still just a bar of soap. Rub the soap over your slightly dampened cloth and rub over sink. Water marks and other greasy stains disappear quickly.

When FEEDING A PET (dog or cat) line the feeding bowl with a piece of aluminum foil and then place the food in it. This will save washing the dish.

If you don't have enough room to STORE BED PILLOWS, select an attractive piece of material that harmonizes with the color scheme of your trailer and make a cover, inserting a zipper either in the end of the case, or across the center of the back. If you wish to add a cording or fringe around the edges, you will have a most attractive throw pillow that can be used on your davenport during the day. At night, unzip, pull out the pillow, and you are ready to make your bed.

When MAKING A TRAILER BED in the morning, do not take off the sheets and blankets, folding each one. Straighten the bed linen, fold up the ends and side nearest you, and roll into a lengthwise roll to the back of the bed. This will slip behind the back cushions of your davenport, and at night it is easy to unroll the bedding and tuck in the foot and front side.

If you have something you do not wish to have riding wildly around in the trailer as you pull down the road, PURCHASE LASHING CORDS (elastic) with hook ends, and secure these to eye screws on the wall or floor. (This is the type of cord commonly used on motor bikes). These will hold folding chairs, TV trays, TV's, etc., firmly in place.

The above-mentioned lashing cords are excellent when installed just above the CLOTHES ROD IN THE CLOSET. Place an eye screw at either end of the rod, just above it, and after all hangers are in place, stretch the elastic cord, hooking it at either end in the eye screw. Hangers will then stay on the rod should you find yourself on a bumpy road. If you do not have these lashing cords, roll a bath towel lengthwise and insert between the rod and the shelf above. You will not find all your clothes on the closet floor after a bumpy session on some back road.

Avoid scouring powder or steel wool for CLEANING GLASSWARE. Soak glass container in soda water to remove burned-on foods.

If your trailer has carpeting and SPILLS occur, tend to the spot as quickly as possible. If a liquid has been spilled, place a bath towel over area, and walk over the spot. The towel will absorb much of the liquid. When one towel becomes saturated, repeat process with another clean towel. Continue until as much as possible has been taken up by the towels. A mixture of 1 part white vinegar to 3 parts water applied to a stain will help to keep the color of the carpeting from being affected by the accident.

III. TOP OF STOVE COOKERY

TOAST

This seems like a very simple thing to include in a cook book, but for a long time I did not know the secret of toast without a toaster. One can always use a toaster when electricity is available, but it is a different story when you are without current to operate simple appliances. I used the old-style toasters that sit on the burner and always produce a dried-out toast, until a trailer friend, Katie Grimm, told me of the very simple method of buttering your bread lightly on both sides and frying it in your Teflon frying pan on top of the stove. It works like a charm, and you will have a few more inches of cabinet space when you no longer carry a toaster.

FRENCH TOAST

1	egg, slightly beaten	¼	teaspoon salt
1	cup milk	2	tablespoons sugar

In a bowl mix the egg, milk, salt and sugar. Dip bread in mixture and brown each side in a well-buttered skillet. Serve with butter and topping such as confectioners sugar or prepared syrup.

Yield: 6 slices

ORANGE FRENCH TOAST

2	eggs, beaten	1	teaspoon cinnamon
3	tablespoons confectioners sugar	2/3	cup orange juice
2	teaspoons grated orange peel	10	slices of bread

Combine all ingredients except bread. Dip bread slices in mixture and brown on both sides on a hot griddle. Serve with powdered sugar, honey or syrup.

Yield: 10 slices

QUICK SKILLET BISCUITS

1   tube refrigerator biscuits   butter

Preheat fry pan or electric skillet. Grease lightly with butter. Place biscuits in pan. Cover and let fry for three minutes. Turn biscuits over and continue frying (covered) for another three to four minutes, or until nicely browned. Serve with jelly or marmalade.   Yield: 10 biscuits

SWEDISH PANCAKES

1½	cups sifted flour	3	eggs
3	tablespoons sugar	2	cups milk
½	teaspoon salt	2	tablespoons melted butter

Sift together in large bowl flour, sugar, and salt. In another bowl beat eggs until thick and cream colored. Blend in milk and butter. Pour egg mixture into dry ingredients and beat until smooth. Heat skillet or griddle. Grease lightly. For each pancake spoon about a tablespoon of batter onto griddle. (Pancakes should be 2½ to 3 inches in diameter). Cook each pancake over medium heat until lightly browned on bottom. Loosen edges with a spatula, turn, and lightly brown second side. As each pancake is cooked, transfer to heated plate. Arrange pancakes in a circle, slightly overlapping each one. Serve with apple sauce or with any syrup desired.   Serves 3-4

POTATO CLAM CHOWDER

2	cans frozen potato soup	1	teaspoon dried parsley flakes
8	ounces minced clams		
	(fresh or canned)		

Prepare soup according to directions on cans, using milk. Add clams together with clam liquid. Heat to serving point. Just before serving sprinkle with parsley flakes.   Serves 4-5

QUICK CREAM OF CORN SOUP

½	teaspoon finely chopped onion	½	teaspoon salt
			dash of pepper
1	tablespoon butter	1	cup cream-style corn
1½	tablespoons flour	2	cups milk

Saute onion in butter. Blend in flour, salt and pepper. Stir over medium heat until smooth. Stir in corn and bring slowly to boil. Let boil for about 1 minute, stirring constantly. Remove from heat and gradually stir in milk. Heat just to serving temperature.

Serves 2-3

CORN CHOWDER

4	slices bacon, diced	2	cups milk
1	onion, thinly sliced		salt
2	cups diced potatoes		pepper
1	package frozen kernel corn (or 1 can kernel corn)		dash of Worcestershire sauce

In heavy skillet fry bacon until crisp. Remove bacon from skillet and fry onion until lightly browned. Add the potatoes and cover with just enough water to simmer. Cook until tender. Add corn, milk, salt, pepper, Worcestershire sauce and bacon bits. Simmer until well blended.

Serves 3-4

SEAFOOD BISQUE

2	cups diced potatoes	1	10-ounce can frozen cream of shrimp soup
2	cups water		
1	10-ounce can frozen condensed oyster stew		

In covered saucepan, cook potatoes in water until tender. Add oyster stew and shrimp soup, heating until completely thawed, stirring occasionally.

Serves 5-6

MUSHROOM CHOW MEIN

2 tablespoons salad oil	3 tablespoons water
2 medium onions, diced	2 tablespoons soy sauce
2 cups hot water	2 No. 1 cans mixed Chinese
2 vegetable bouillon cubes	vegetables, drained and rinsed
3 tablespoons cornstarch	with cold water
2 teaspoons sugar	8 ounces mushrooms,
salt to taste	fresh or canned
1 teaspoon Accent	1 5-ounce can water chestnuts,
½ teaspoon dry mustard	drained and sliced
⅛ teaspoon pepper	1 canned pimento, cut in strips

Heat oil in large skillet. Then saute onions for 5 minutes, stirring frequently. Add hot water and bouillon cubes, stirring until cubes are dissolved. Blend together cornstarch, sugar, salt, Accent, mustard, pepper, water, and soy sauce and stir into onion mixture. Cook until thick and clear. Add remaining ingredients, stirring gently until just heated through. Serve over hot Chinese noodles or hot rice. Have more soy sauce on hand.   Serves 5-6

NOTE: Occasionally, I brown strips of round steak or chuck fillets with the onions. This makes a heartier Chow Mein.

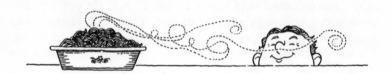

YAKIMESHI (FRIED RICE)

3 tablespoons peanut oil	4 cups cooked rice
(or salad oil)	3-4 tablespoons soy sauce
1 egg	salt and pepper
½ pound cooked pork, chicken	1 bunch green onions, chopped
or ham, cubed	(use tops also)

Heat oil in frying pan. Add egg and scramble. Add meat, rice, soy sauce, salt and pepper. Heat thoroughly. Add onions and cook another 2 minutes. (A good pot-luck dish!)   Serves 4-5

FIFTEEN-MINUTE CHICKEN CHOW MEIN

2	tablespoons peanut or salad oil	¾	teaspoon salt
½	cup sliced onion	⅛	teaspoon pepper
1½	cups diagonally sliced celery	⅛	teaspoon ginger
1	No. 2 can chop suey vegetables	1	tablespoon brown sugar
		1	tablespoon cornstarch
1	cup drained pineapple tidbits	2	tablespoons soy sauce
1	chicken bouillon cube, dissolved in ¼ cup boiling water	1	cup diced, cooked chicken

In a heavy skillet, heat oil. Add onions and celery. Drain liquid from vegetables and replace with fresh water to top of can. Add this to skillet. Continue cooking. Add pineapple, dissolved bouillon cube, salt, pepper, ginger, and brown sugar. Cover and bring to a boil. Mix cornstarch with soy sauce and stir into first mixture. Cook, stirring until thickened (about 5 minutes). Add chicken, and heat to serving temperature. Serve over noodles or cooked rice.

Serves 3-4

PERFECT BEEF STEW

¼	cup flour	1	bay leaf, crushed
¾	teaspoon salt	1	No. 303 can tomatoes
¼	teaspoon Lawry's salt pepper to taste	2	medium potatoes, cut into bite-size pieces
1	pound beef, cubed	4	carrots, cut in pieces
2	tablespoons shortening	4	stalks celery, cut
1	small onion, diced	1	small can mushrooms

In heavy paper bag, mix flour, salts and pepper. Drop in pieces of beef and shake to coat. Heat shortening in skillet. Brown meat and onion. Blend in any remaining flour mixture. Add bay leaf and tomatoes. Cover and simmer approximately 1¼ hours (or until meat is tender). Add potatoes and vegetables and continue to simmer another 20-25 minutes. Add mushrooms. (If gravy is too thin, thicken with mixture of flour and water.)

Serves 4-5

PORCUPINES (A ONE-POT RECIPE)

From Camp-Fire-Girl campouts comes this recipe:

1	pound ground beef	1	teaspoon salt
1	cup instant rice		dash of pepper
1	small onion, chopped	2	10-ounce cans tomato soup
1	egg, beaten slightly with fork	2	soup cans of water

Combine meat, rice, onion, egg, and seasonings. Shape into balls. Pour soup and water into skillet, stirring and heating until it reaches boiling point. Add meat balls. Cover and simmer 40 minutes.

Serves 4-5

SWEDISH MEAT BALLS

1	pound ground round steak	1	small onion, diced
½	pound pork shoulder, ground		salt and pepper to taste
½	cup bread crumbs	½	teaspoon allspice
1	egg		dash of nutmeg
½	cup water	3	tablespoons butter

Lightly mix together all ingredients in a large bowl. Shape mixture into balls about 1 inch in diameter. Heat butter in skillet and over low heat brown meat balls on all sides. Shake pan frequently to brown evenly and to keep balls round. Cover and cook about 15 minutes over low heat until meat balls are thoroughly cooked. Make pan gravy from any meat drippings left in the pan.

Serves 4

ITALIAN SPAGHETTI AND MEAT BALLS

½	cup minced onion	2	cups water
3	tablespoons shortening	1	tablespoon salt
2	No. 1 cans tomatoes	1	tablespoon sugar
1	6-ounce can tomato paste	½	teaspoon pepper
1	can tomato soup		pinch of anise seed
1	teaspoon oregano		

In skillet brown onion in fat. Then add remaining ingredients. Simmer for 1 hour. Meanwhile prepare meat balls:

¾	pound ground beef	½	cup grated Parmesan cheese
¼	pound ground pork	1	tablespoon parsley flakes
	(or mild sausage)	½	cup milk
1	cup fine dry bread crumbs	2	eggs, well beaten

Mix all the ingredients together well, then form into balls and brown in separate, small skillet. Add meat balls to sauce. Simmer for 1 hour. Cook one package of spaghetti according to directions on package. Serve meat ball sauce over spaghetti.   Serves 4-5

QUICK CHILI

1	can bean and bacon soup	1	10½-ounce can chili with beans
1	can tomato soup	1¼	cups water

Combine above ingredients and simmer for 10 minutes.

Serves 4

TASTY SUPPER CASSEROLE

1	pound ground beef	¼	cup slivered almonds
¾	cup raw brown rice	1	cup chopped celery
1	package onion soup mix	2	cups water (approximately)

Brown hamburger in hot skillet. Add remaining ingredients. Cover and simmer gently about 1 hour, or until rice is cooked. Should it appear a bit dry, add a little more water. (This recipe can also be baked in a covered casserole, in a 275 degree oven for 1½ hours.)   Serves 4-5

JIFFY MEAT-BALL STEW

2	tablespoons shortening		Accent
1	cup Minute rice	1	can cream of mushroom soup
½	envelope onion soup mix	1	soup can of water
1-1½	pounds ground beef		

In a large flat baking dish or heavy skillet, melt the shortening. Remove from stove and spread rice and onion soup mix evenly over bottom of dish. Shape ground beef into 5 or 6 patties and lay them on top of rice mixture. Sprinkle with Accent. Mix mushroom soup and water in a small bowl until smooth. Pour over meat and rice. Cover skillet and simmer over low heat 45 minutes, or until meat is cooked through and rice is tender.

Serves 4-5

BROILED BEEFETTES

1	pound lean ground beef	1	teaspoon baking powder
3	tablespoons onion soup mix		salt and pepper
½	cup milk		

Combine all ingredients, blending thoroughly. (In measuring out the onion soup mix, make sure the contents of package have been well blended.) Salt and pepper to taste. Shape mixture into 4 to 6 patties. Broil in oven or over charcoal. (The addition of baking powder makes a light fluffy hamburger patty.)   Serves 4

BEEF STROGANOFF

4	pounds boneless beef, cut in strips	3	cans beef consomme
		8	ounces mushrooms (fresh or canned)
1	cup flour		
2	teaspoons salt	6	tablespoons butter
1	teaspoon Accent	2	cups sour cream
¼	teaspoon pepper	6	tablespoons tomato paste
2/3	cup butter	2	teaspoons Worcestershire sauce
1	cup chopped onion		

Dredge meat with a mixture of the flour, salt, Accent, and pepper. Heat butter in skillet and brown meat with onions. Add consomme. Cover and simmer about 20 minutes. In small fry pan, saute mushrooms in butter. Add them to meat mixture. Blend together sour cream, tomato paste, and Worcestershire sauce. Remove meat from burner and add sour cream mixture. Place skillet over a very slow heat until it reaches serving temperature, being careful not to let it boil. Serves 10

NOTE: If you wish to freeze the Stroganoff, cool quickly, and pop into freezer. To serve, defrost at room temperature, and heat very slowly to prevent any separation of ingredients. It can also be brought to serving temperature in 350 degree oven for 30 minutes, if you prefer that method of heating.

TRAILER STEW

A hearty one-dish meal, the ingredients of which may be determined by your family's tastes and the contents of your cupboard. While frozen vegetables are a bit more desirable, canned vegetables may be substituted.

2	tablespoons butter	4	medium potatoes
2	pounds ground beef	½	package frozen green beans
½	package onion soup mix	½	package frozen corn
4	medium carrots		salt and pepper to taste

Heat butter in heavy skillet or kettle over your campfire or stove in the trailer and brown the meat. Add soup mix. Add raw vegetables first, covering with water and cooking covered until vegetables are almost tender. Then add frozen vegetables and cook until all are tender. Serve in bowls. Serves 5-6

BRAISED BEEF AND NOODLES

2	pounds round steak, cut in strips flour	2 ½ 1	8-ounce cans tomato sauce cup grape juice teaspoon Accent
2	tablespoons butter	½	teaspoon (more or less) oregano
1	medium onion, diced		salt and pepper to taste
½	cup water	1	package noodles, cooked

Dredge meat lightly with flour. Brown with onion in butter. Add all other ingredients except noodles, and simmer gently, covered, stirring occasionally for 1½ hours, or until meat is tender. As gravy cooks down, it might be necessary to add a little more water. Serve in center of noodle ring, or over boiled and buttered noodles.   Serves 5-6

CREAMED CHIPPED BEEF AND MUSHROOMS

1	4-ounce jar chipped beef, shredded	⅛ 2	teaspoon pepper cups milk
¼	cup butter	1	small can mushrooms, drained
¼	cup flour		

If dried beef appears to be very salty, pour boiling water over it and let it stand for a few minutes. Drain off water. Saute beef in butter until edges curl. Blend in flour and pepper. (Do not add salt, as chipped beef will provide necessary salt.) Gradually add milk and bring to a boil over medium heat, stirring constantly. Add mushrooms and serve over hot rice or buttered toast pieces.
                                Serves 3-4

QUICK ONE-PAN MEAL

1	12-ounce can luncheon meat butter	1 ¼	No. 1 can cream style corn teaspoon salt
3	eggs, slightly beaten		dash pepper

Cube luncheon meat and brown it in a little butter in skillet. Combine remaining ingredients. Add this to meat. Cook over low heat, stirring occasionally, until the eggs have set. Do not let it reach a "dry" stage.   Serves 4

NOTE: There can be variations of this recipe also — add bits of chopped green pepper, mushrooms, pimento, etc.

NOODLES DELUXE

1	8-ounce package noodles	½	cup small curd cottage cheese
2	tablespoons butter	1	cup sour cream
1	medium onion, minced		

Cook noodles as directed on package. Drain. In butter, saute onion. Add cottage cheese, sour cream and noodles, and heat only to serving temperature. Season with salt and pepper to taste.

Serves 4-5

SHRIMP CREOLE

In a large skillet melt 2 tablespoons butter. Fry ½ cup minced onion until it appears transparent. Then blend in:

2	tablespoons flour	½	cup diced green pepper
1	bay leaf, crushed	½	teaspoon salt
¼	cup diced celery	1	6-ounce can tomato paste
1	teaspoon minced parsley	2½	cups water

Cook slowly, stirring occasionally until thickened, about 30 minutes. Stir in 2 cups cooked shrimp (about 14 ounces, if using canned shrimp). Serve over warm, buttered rice. If you want it to be "party like," pack cooked rice into a greased bowl while warm, invert onto serving dish, garnish with parsley, and surround with shrimp.

Serves 4-5

EASY OMELET

3	tablespoons butter	¼	cup milk
6	eggs		salt and pepper to taste

Melt butter in skillet while preparing eggs. Break eggs into bowl, add milk and salt and pepper to taste. Beat lightly with beater or fork. Pour into melted butter. Cover and cook over low heat until lightly cooked, but not hard on top. With a spatula, fold half of omelet over other half. Cut into 4 wedges and serve. Omelet can be varied by adding cheese, jelly, crumbled bacon bits, etc., before folding over.

Serves 3

QUICK CHICKEN-AND-RICE DINNER

In the upper portion of the double boiler (but **not** over boiling water) prepare 4 servings of minute rice according to directions on package. After rice has steamed, place pan over boiling water and add:

1 cube butter (½ cup)	2 6-ounce cans boneless chicken
1 8-ounce can mushrooms	chopped parsley

Heat, covered, for 15 minutes. If you feel this is a bit dry, dissolve 1 chicken bouillon cube in 1 cup hot water and pour over the ingredients. Sprinkle with parsley. (If fresh parsley is not available, use dried parsley flakes.)   Serves 4-5

HAWAIIAN BAKED BEANS

1 No. 1 can New England	1 tablespoon syrup from pineapple
style baked beans	1 tablespoon ketchup
2½ tablespoons brown sugar	1 teaspoon prepared mustard
1 No. 2 can pineapple chunks,	
drained of most of syrup	

Mix together until well blended in attractive flameproof serving dish. Heat until flavors have mixed, and it is bubbling.

Serves 4

QUICK BEAN CASSEROLE

1 small onion, minced	2 tablespoons brown sugar
4 slices bacon, diced	¾ teaspoon mustard
2 cans baked beans (brick oven	¼ teaspoon Worcestershire sauce
variety)	

In flameproof casserole or skillet, saute onion and bacon. Then add remaining ingredients. Stir together and heat slowly over low flame until mixture reaches a bubbly stage. Serve with Boston Brown Bread.   Serves 5

SKILLET POTATO SALAD

6	slices bacon	½	teaspoon salt
1	can cream of celery soup	1	tablespoon chopped pimento
2	tablespoons sweet pickle relish	1	pound can sliced potatoes,
2	teaspoons onion flakes		drained
4	teaspoons vinegar		frankfurters

Fry bacon until crisp. Remove bacon and crumble into bits. Pour off fat from skillet, allowing approximately 1 tablespoon to remain. Blend in soup, relish, onion, vinegar, salt and pimento. Heat to boiling point. Gently stir in potatoes. Place desired number of frankfurters on top, cover and heat about 10 minutes, or until heated through.   Serves 5-6

COMPANY HAM

4	tablespoons butter	1	can mushroom soup
¼	cup chopped onion	2	cups sour cream
2	cups chopped, cooked ham	1	8-ounce can mushrooms, drained
4	teaspoons flour		hot, cooked rice or noodles

Melt butter in large skillet. Add onion and ham. Saute until onion is transparent. Sprinkle in flour. Stir soup until it is smooth and then blend it into ham mixture. Cook over moderate heat a few minutes. Gradually stir in sour cream. Add mushrooms. Continue to cook until mixture is just heated through. (Do not let it reach boiling point.) Serve over rice or noodles. Garnish with fresh chopped parsley or parsley flakes.   Serves 6

WILD RICE CASSEROLE

This is favorite party fare. However, with the present high price of wild rice, two 6-ounce packages of Uncle Ben's mixed Long Grain and Wild Rice may be successfully substituted. If you do this, follow package directions to cook rice. Otherwise follow directions below:

1	cup wild rice	1	medium onion, diced
2	tablespoons butter	1	green pepper, diced
2	tablespoons water	1	large can mushrooms
1	bunch celery, chopped	1	cup light cream

Wash wild rice in strainer, allowing water to run through it thoroughly. Boil rice in salted water 45 minutes. Drain water and replace lid to let rice steam and plump for a few minutes.

Meanwhile in skillet, melt butter and water. In this, simmer the celery, onion and green pepper until they are just tender. (Do not overcook.) Then add the rice, mushrooms and cream. Season with salt to taste. Heat to serving temperature, but do not allow to reach boiling stage. This can be kept warm, and if mixture needs a bit more moisture, more cream can be added. This sure hit recipe is at home served with ham, beef, or poultry. Serves 5-6

GLAZED FRUIT SALAD

This is a delightful fruit salad, made almost completely from items on the pantry shelf. It is a recipe that lends itself to substitutions should there be some fruits that you would prefer using.

1	No. 1 can fruit cocktail (or fruits for salad)	7	bananas, sliced
1	No. 1 can pineapple chunks	1	can apricot pie filling
2	11-ounce cans mandarin oranges	2	tablespoons lemon juice

Drain fruit and place in mixing bowl. Blend in thoroughly the pie filling and lemon juice. Chill for several hours before serving. Line your favorite bowl with cupped lettuce leaves and spoon fruit salad carefully into bowl. This makes a rather large salad.

Serves 8-10

NOTE: Should you not have the bananas on hand, marshmallows and coconut are especially good substitutes.

QUICK FRUIT MOLD

2 packages orange jello (6 ounces)	1 8-ounce can crushed pineapple
1 No. 1 can cranberry sauce	2 7-ounce bottles gingerale or Seven-Up

Combine jello and cranberry sauce in a saucepan. Heat and stir until jello is dissolved. Remove from heat and add pineapple and gingerale. When foam has disappeared, pour into mold and chill. Unmold and garnish with drained grapefruit and orange slices or any fruit, fresh or canned, that you have available.

Serves 8

ALMOND ORANGE SALAD

A tasty salad with a very subtle flavor. It makes a lovely salad for the fall season when you are thinking of fall colors for your table.

1 3-ounce package lemon jello	2 11-ounce cans mandarin oranges
1 tablespoon vinegar	½ cup slivered almonds, blanched
1 tablespoon ketchup	

Drain oranges, reserving the liquid. Add enough water to make 2 cups. Heat about half of this and dissolve the jello in it. Add the remaining liquid. Stir in vinegar and ketchup. Chill until partially set. Add oranges and almonds. Pour into an 8x8 pan or into a ring mold, or in individual molds.   Serves 6

NOTE: As a dressing for this salad, mix equal parts of mayonnaise and whipped cream, or blend a bit of honey into mayonnaise.

SPICY APRICOT SALAD

1½	cups apricot nectar	1	envelope unflavored gelatin
¼	cup lemon juice	2	tablespoons cold water
1	teaspoon prepared mustard	¼	cup mayonnaise
		3	tablespoons chopped green pepper
2	tablespoons sugar	½	cup crushed pineapple, drained
¼	teaspoon celery salt		

In a saucepan combine nectar, lemon juice, mustard, sugar and celery salt. Heat to almost boiling point. Meanwhile soften gelatin in cold water. Remove apricot nectar mixture from stove and add gelatin. Stir until dissolved. Cool until it begins to thicken, then add mayonnaise. (If this does not become smooth and creamy, take a few turns with your egg beater to give it a smooth texture.) Add green pepper and pineapple. Pour into one mold, or 7 individual molds.

SKILLET FRENCH FRIES

Place 1 package frozen french fries in a large skillet. Pour in just enough cooking oil to cover and stir until pieces are well coated. Make sure they are in a single layer. Over a medium heat, cook 12 or 13 minutes, stirring occasionally. Remove when brown and drain on paper toweling. Sprinkle with salt before serving.

Serves 3

ONE-PAN — ONE-STEP POTATOES

4	medium potatoes, peeled & diced	1	teaspoon salt
			dash of pepper
2	tablespoons butter	1	teaspoon grated Parmesan cheese
1	cup milk		

Combine all ingredients in a two-quart saucepan. Simmer over a low heat, covered, 15 to 20 minutes, or until potatoes are tender. Stir occasionally to keep them from sticking.   Serves 4-5

EASY CREAMED VEGETABLES

2   packages frozen vegetables
1   can cream of vegetable, celery, mushroom, or chicken soup

Cook vegetables in unsalted water until tender. Drain. Stir in soup of your choice. Heat to serving temperature. (If sauce appears to be too thick, thin to desired consistency with milk.) Season to taste.

Serves 6-8

FOR GLAZED CARROTS

¼   cup cranberry jelly   ¼   cup brown sugar
¼   cup butter

Combine ingredients and pour over carrots, stirring just until thoroughly coated.

Serves 4-5

CHEESE-SEASONED POTATOES

1   tablespoon butter   1   teaspoon Parmesan cheese
1   No. 1 can potatoes   parsley (optional)
1   teaspoon Lawry's seasoned salt

Melt butter in a Corning Ware dish or small skillet. Add the potatoes and seasonings. Heat over low heat, stirring occasionally. Just before serving sprinkle with chopped parsley or parsley flakes. (These potatoes can also be done in a moderate oven, should you have your oven going for some other part of the meal. Or they may be popped under the broiler for a few minutes, until butter and seasonings have blended with potatoes and they are slightly browned.)

Serves 3-4

CORN ON THE COB

While many people just "boil" corn, it often turns out to be tough and it need not be. Corn should not be overcooked. The best way to cook it is to drop the husked ears into boiling water. Bring the water to a boil again and boil no longer than 5 minutes. A pinch of sugar may be added to the water, but never salt the water. Salt will toughen the corn.

SKILLET COOKIES

A prized Maryland recipe from two sisters, Miriam Brooks and Vi Merrill. In addition to being a delightful cookie, it is one of the few that can be made without an oven.

¼	pound butter (1 stick)	2	cups Rice Krispies
¾	cup sugar	½	cup chopped nuts
½	pound dates, chopped	1	teaspoon vanilla
2	egg yolks		powdered sugar

Combine butter, sugar, dates and egg yolks in saucepan and cook for about 10 minutes over medium heat, stirring constantly to keep mixture from sticking to bottom of pan. Remove from heat and stir in remaining ingredients. When well blended, and while mixture is still warm, working with 2 teaspoons, form into clusters or balls about 1 inch in diameter. Drop into a plastic bag containing about 1 cup powdered sugar. After you have put in 7 or 8 balls, hold the bag shut and shake lightly to coat them. Remove balls to a piece of waxed paper. Repeat process until all batter is made into cookies.　　　　　Yield: 2 to 3 dozen

CHOW MEIN COOKIES

1	package chocolate chips	2	3-ounce cans chow mein noodles
1	package butterscotch chips		

In double boiler (over boiling water) melt chocolate chips and butterscotch chips. Add chow mein noodles. Form into balls and drop onto waxed paper. Chill until set.　　　　　Yield: 3-4 dozen

NOTE: If you do not happen to have chow mein noodles, 2 cans shoe string potatoes can be substituted.

KRISPIE BARS

½	cup white Karo syrup	3	cups Rice Krispies
½	cup sugar	1½	cups chocolate chips
¾	cup peanut butter		

In saucepan combine syrup and sugar. Bring just to boiling point over medium heat. Then add peanut butter and Rice Krispies. Pat into 9x12 pan. Frost with melted chocolate chips. Cut into squares while warm.　　　　　Yield: 4 dozen

THREE-LAYER BARS

This recipe makes a "melt in your mouth" bar which requires no baking.

½	cup butter	¼	cup butter
½	cup sugar	2	tablespoons milk
5	tablespoons cocoa	2	cups powdered sugar
1	egg, slightly beaten	2	tablespoons instant vanilla
1	teaspoon vanilla		pudding mix
2	cups graham cracker crumbs	1	teaspoon lemon juice
½	cup walnuts, chopped	5	squares semisweet chocolate
1	cup angel flake coconut	1	tablespoon butter

LAYER I:

In top of double boiler, melt and stir butter, sugar, and cocoa until slightly thickened. Remove pan from hot water and add egg and vanilla. When blended, add graham cracker crumbs, walnuts, and coconut. Pat mixture into bottom of 9x12 pan. Chill.

LAYER II:

In another bowl, cream butter, milk, powdered sugar, pudding mix, and lemon juice. When mixture is smooth and well blended, spread over graham cracker mixture and again chill.

LAYER III:

Melt chocolate and butter in top of double boiler over boiling water. Spread over the first two layers and when it has cooled slightly, before chocolate has become firm, cut into rather small squares. Chill in refrigerator just long enough to harden chocolate. (These bars freeze very well.)   Yield: 4-5 dozen

NO BAKE CHOCOLATE CLUSTERS

1	pound sweet chocolate	2	cups cornflakes
2	squares unsweetened	1	cup walnuts chopped
	chocolate	1	cup coconut

In top of double boiler, melt sweet chocolate and unsweetened chocolate. Then add remaining ingredients. Mix until blended. Drop by teaspoons onto waxed paper. Chill in refrigerator until set.   Yield: 3-4 dozen

QUICK FRUIT TAPIOCA

An easy, refreshing dessert from items usually kept on the pantry shelf. To "party" it up a bit, add a dab of whipped cream or whipped topping.

1	No. 303 can fruit for salads	¼	teaspoon cinnamon
4	tablespoons brown sugar	1	teaspoon lemon juice
	dash of salt	1/3	cup raisins (optional)
2	tablespoons Minute Tapioca		

Drain fruit, reserving liquid. Add water to liquid to make 1½ cups. In a saucepan combine brown sugar, salt, tapioca, cinnamon and lemon juice. Gradually stir in the 1½ cups of liquid. Cook, stirring constantly until it reaches a rolling boil. Boil for a minute or so. Stir in fruit and raisins. (If the fruit is in very large pieces, you may want to cut it a bit smaller.) Let stand 15 minutes. Serve warm or cold.   Serves 4

STOVE TOP LEMON SOUFFLE

An easy recipe for a light, fluffy lemon souffle with its own rich lemon sauce.

2	eggs		dash of salt
1	cup sugar	3	tablespoons lemon juice
1	tablespoon flour		cinnamon
1	cup milk		

Separate eggs, placing yolks in the top part of the double boiler, and the whites in a small bowl. Beat the egg whites until stiff. In the top of the double boiler, beat the egg yolks, adding sugar, flour, milk, salt, and lemon juice. Stir until well blended. Fold in the beaten egg whites. Shake a bit of cinnamon over the top. Cover. Cook one hour over gently boiling water, being careful not to lift the cover (not even to peek). Serve warm.   Serves 4

SWEDISH SNOW PUDDING

A very light fluffy pudding with a refreshing lemon flavor.

2	envelopes Knox unflavored gelatin	1½	cups sugar
		½	cup lemon juice
½	cup cold water	3	stiffly beaten egg whites
2	cups hot water		

In a medium size mixing bowl, soften gelatin in cold water. Then add hot water and stir until dissolved. Add sugar, continuing to stir until sugar is dissolved. Add lemon juice. Chill until partially set. Beat until frothy. Fold in beaten egg whites. Mold in refrigerator until firm. Serve cold with the following:

CUSTARD SAUCE

3	beaten egg yolks	2	cups scalded milk
	dash of salt	1	teaspoon vanilla
¼	cup sugar		

In the top of the double boiler, combine beaten egg yolks with salt and sugar. Gradually stir in scalded milk. Cook over hot water until mixture coats spoon, stirring constantly. Remove from heat. Add vanilla. Chill thoroughly.   Serves 6-8

PUMPKIN CHIFFON PIE

3	egg yolks	½	teaspoon nutmeg
½	cup sugar	1	tablespoon unflavored gelatin
1¼	cups pumpkin	¼	cup cold water
½	cup milk	3	egg whites
½	teaspoon salt	½	cup sugar
½	teaspoon ginger		whipped cream
½	teaspoon cinnamon		

Beat egg yolks, sugar, pumpkin, milk, salt and spices. Cook until thick. Soften gelatin in cold water and add to hot pumpkin mixture, stirring to be sure gelatin is dissolved. Cool. Beat egg whites and sugar until stiff. Fold cool pumpkin into egg-white mixture and turn into a baked pie shell. Chill until firm. Top with whipped cream.   Serves 6

SWEDISH FRUIT SOUP

1	box mixed dried fruits (No. 1 size)	1	3-inch stick of cinnamon
½	cup raisins	1	teaspoon grated orange rind
¼	cup sugar	1	package frozen raspberries, partially thawed
3	tablespoons quick cooking tapioca		whipped cream
			slivered almonds

With a sharp knife, remove pits from prunes and cut pears and peaches into smaller pieces. Place dried fruits and next 4 ingredients in saucepan and cover with 2 quarts water. Bring to a boil, reduce heat, cover and simmer about 1 hour, or until fruit is tender. Stir a few times during cooking period to be sure fruit is not sticking to pan. Remove from heat and add raspberries. Stir gently until all is blended. Serve fruit soup either warm or cold, topped with whipped cream and slivered almonds.   Serves 6-8

NOTE: If you desire a rosy appearance to fruit soup, add a few drops of red food coloring.

FRESH STRAWBERRY PIE

3½	cups sugar	2	teaspoons butter
¾	cup boiling water	½	teaspoon liquid red food coloring
4	heaping tablespoons cornstarch	1	quart fresh strawberries
½	cup cold water	2	baked pie shells
			whipped cream

In saucepan, dissolve sugar in boiling water. In a separate bowl, dissolve cornstarch in cold water. Add to first mixture. Bring to boiling point and cook until mixture is thickened. Remove from stove and add butter and food coloring. Cool. Clean and hull strawberries and place them in pie shells. Pour cooked glaze over berries and allow to thoroughly cool. Serve with whipped cream.   Serves 12

CHOCOLATE BAVARIAN CREAM

For years this has remained my husband's favorite dessert.

18	chocolate Oreo cookies	½	cup sugar
1/3	cup melted butter	¼	teaspoon salt
1	tablespoon unflavored gelatin	1	cup milk
		1	teaspoon vanilla
¼	cup cold water	3	egg whites, stiffly beaten
3	egg yolks, slightly beaten	1	cup heavy cream whipped

Place cookies between two sheets of waxed paper and crush with rolling pin. Combine crushed cookies and melted butter and press into a 9 inch pie plate. Chill. Then prepare custard:

In a small bowl, soften gelatin in cold water and set aside. In top of double boiler combine egg yolks with sugar and salt. Gradually add milk. Cook, stirring constantly, over boiling water until mixture coats the spoon (about 5 minutes), or until the white streaks on top of the mixture disappear. Remove from stove.

Add softened gelatin and stir until dissolved. Cool. When room temperature, add vanilla. Fold in egg whites and whipped cream. Pour into chocolate crust. Grate unsweetened chocolate curls over top of pie. Chill until ready to serve. (This recipe may be prepared the day before you wish to serve it.)   Serves 6-8

The following blank pages are for your own use.

IV. USING YOUR OVEN

SWEDISH RYE BREAD

This is a family "heirloom" in the Strom household:

2	cups milk	2	cups Karo syrup
1	cup liquid shortening		(dark, blue label)
2	packages dry yeast	3	cups white flour
1	teaspoon sugar	2	cups rye flour
1	cup lukewarm water		grated orange rind
1	teaspoon salt	4-5	cups white flour

Scald milk and pour into mixing bowl to cool. Add liquid shortening. In a small dish, dissolve yeast and sugar in lukewarm water. When milk has reached lukewarm stage, add salt, Karo syrup, 3 cups white flour, 2 cups rye flour, the yeast mixture, and grated orange rind. Mix well, beating until smooth. Then add the rest of the white flour, beating in as much as possible with your mixer, then adding the rest beating by hand.

On floured board, knead for approximately 10 minutes, or until the dough feels smooth and satiny. Place in large greased bowl, and allow to rise until double in bulk, or until a fingerprint will remain when finger is pushed into dough. On floured board, divide dough into 4 portions. Shape each piece into a loaf, place in bread pan, and allow to rise again until double. Bake in 350 degree oven approximately 40 minutes. Remove one loaf pan and tap lightly on bottom of loaf. If tapping produces a hollow sound, the bread is done.   Yield: 4 loaves

SWEDISH "THIEF BOY" ROLLS

So named by Swedish women years ago because the rolls "stole" all their butter. The favorite sweet roll in our family.

1½	packages dry yeast	¾	cup scalded milk
1	teaspoon sugar	5	cups flour (approximately)
¼	cup warm water	3	eggs, beaten
½	cup butter	1	cup butter, melted
½	cup sugar	2	cups sugar
1	teaspoon salt		ground walnuts or pecans

Dissolve yeast and sugar in water. Combine the ½ cup butter, ½ cup sugar and salt in scalded milk. Cool to lukewarm. Add yeast mixture and beat well.

Add 2 cups of the flour, beating until smooth. Beat in eggs and remaining flour. This makes a soft dough. Knead lightly for 3 or 4 minutes until dough is smooth and satiny. Place in greased bowl and let rise until double in bulk (about 1 hour). Divide dough into fourths. Shape each piece into a 12-inch roll. Cut each roll into 12 pieces. Shape each piece into a 7-inch rope, dip into butter, then sugar, and again in melted butter, then nuts. Fold the 7-inch rope in half and twist. Place on greased cookie sheet. Cover. Allow to rise until double (20-30 minutes). Bake in 350 degree oven 15 to 20 minutes, until nicely browned.

Yield: 48 rolls

SWEDISH COFFEE BRAIDS

1	cup milk	3½-4½	cups presifted flour
½	cup sugar	1/3	cup soft butter
½	teaspoon salt	1	cup raisins
1½	teaspoons cardamom	1	egg, slightly beaten
2	packages dry yeast	1/3	cup crushed loaf sugar
¼	cup warm water	1/3	cup chopped almonds

Scald milk. Add to sugar, salt and cardamom in mixing bowl. Cool to lukewarm. Soften yeast in water. Add to first mixture. Stir in one half of the flour and beat until smooth. Stir in butter and raisins, then remaining flour. Knead on floured board until smooth. Place in greased bowl and let rise 50-60 minutes, or until an impression remains when finger is pushed into dough. Punch down. Let rise again 15 minutes. Divide dough into thirds. Make each of these portions into 3 strands and braid. Cover and let rise 30 minutes. Brush braids with slightly beaten egg. Sprinkle with crushed lump sugar and almonds. Bake in 350 degree oven for 25-30 minutes.

PEG BOWDEN'S DILLY BREAD

1	package dry yeast	2	teaspoons dill seed
¼	cup warm water	1	teaspoon salt
1	cup small curd cottage cheese	¼	teaspoon soda
	(heated to lukewarm)	1	unbeaten egg
2	tablespoons sugar	2¼-2½	cups Wondra (instant)
1	tablespoon instant minced		flour
	onion		butter
1	tablespoon butter		garlic salt

Soften dry yeast in warm water. Combine in mixing bowl cottage cheese, sugar, onion, butter, dill seed, salt, soda, egg and the yeast mixture. Beat well until blended. Add flour and beat until it forms a stiff dough. Cover and let rise until double in bulk (50-60 minutes). Stir down. Turn into a well-greased angel food pan. Let rise 30-40 minutes. Bake in 350 degree oven for 40 minutes. Remove from oven, brush with butter and garlic salt. Cool and slice into pieces. When serving, wrap in foil and reheat in slow oven until heated through.

CRANBERRY ORANGE BREAD

2	cups flour	2/3	cup orange juice
1	cup sugar	1	tablespoon grated orange rind
1½	teaspoons baking powder	1	cup chopped nuts
½	teaspoon soda	1	cup cranberries, chopped fine
3	tablespoons butter		or ground
1	egg, beaten		

Sift dry ingredients. Cut in butter until mixture looks like coarse corn meal. Add egg and orange juice. Blend in rind, nuts, and cranberries. Turn into loaf pan. Bake in 350 degree oven for 1 hour.

MARY HUTTON'S BRAN MUFFINS

This recipe comes from a friend in Sheridan, Wyoming. It makes one of the most delicious muffins I have ever tasted. The dough will keep for at least a month in a covered plastic container in the refrigerator — that is, if you can keep it that long. You can be serving muffins right from the oven in a matter of minutes for either breakfast or a snack.

1¼	cups sugar	2	cups bran buds soaked in
½	cup plus 1½ tablespoons		1 cup boiling water
	margarine	3	cups flour
½	quart buttermilk	2½	teaspoons baking soda
2	eggs	1	teaspoon salt
1	cup all bran		

Cream together the sugar and softened margarine. Then add buttermilk and mix well. Add remaining ingredients, mix together well, and chill in refrigerator before baking. Bake in 400 degree oven for 16-19 minutes.   Yield: 3 dozen

BUTTERHORN REFRIGERATOR ROLLS

1	cake yeast	1	cup lukewarm milk
1	tablespoon sugar	¼	teaspoon salt
¼	cup soft butter	4	cups flour
½	cup sugar	2	tablespoons melted butter
3	eggs, beaten		

Work the yeast and sugar together with a spoon until liquid. Set aside. In mixing bowl, cream together butter and sugar. Then add the eggs, milk, salt, and yeast mixture. Gradually add the flour and work until smooth. Place dough in greased bowl, cover, and refrigerate overnight or for at least 8 hours before shaping into rolls.

About 2½ hours before you are ready to bake rolls, remove dough from refrigerator and shape into rolls. Divide into three parts. Roll each part into a circle approximately 12 inches in diameter. With a knife, cut each circle of dough into 16 wedge-shaped pieces. With a pastry brush, brush with butter, then roll each wedge, starting at the outside (large) edge, working toward center of circle. Place on greased cookie sheet. Brush tops with more melted butter. Cover and let rise 2 to 2½ hours. Bake in 375 degree oven for 8 minutes, or until nicely browned. (These rolls freeze well and can be reheated in pan covered with foil in very slow oven.) Yield: 48 rolls

APPLESAUCE BREAD

1	egg, well beaten	1 tablespoon baking powder
1	cup applesauce	1 teaspoon salt
2	tablespoons melted shortening (not butter)	½ teaspoon baking soda
		½ teaspoon cinnamon
2	cups sifted flour	1 cup coarsely chopped nuts
¾	cup sugar	

Blend together beaten egg and applesauce. Add shortening. Sift together all dry ingredients and add to first mixture. Add chopped nuts and stir until just blended. Turn into greased bread loaf pan. Bake in 350 degree oven for 1 hour.

LEILA WILSON'S PUMPKIN BREAD

Another Sheridan, Wyoming recipe for a moist, rich bread that freezes well and will keep for a week at least in your refrigerator.

1 2/3	cups flour	1/3	cup butter, softened
1 2/3	cups sugar	1/3	cup water
¼	teaspoon baking powder	1	cup pumpkin
1	teaspoon soda	2	eggs
¾	teaspoon salt	1/3	cup chopped nuts
½	teaspoon cinnamon	2/3	cup raisins
¼	teaspoon ground cloves		

Sift together flour, sugar, baking powder, soda, salt, cinnamon and cloves. Cream together softened butter, water, pumpkin, and eggs. Gradually add dry ingredients. Then add nuts and raisins. Bake in greased loaf pan in 350 degree oven for 50-60 minutes. (If you are using two smaller pans, bake for 45-50 minutes).

CORN BREAD OR MUFFINS

1	tablespoon melted butter	1½	cups flour
½	cup sugar	½	cup corn meal
1	egg	3	teaspoons baking powder
1	cup milk	¼	teaspoon salt

Mix melted butter, sugar and egg well. Then add dry ingredients alternately with milk. Bake in greased 9x9x2 pan or in muffin tins in 375 degree oven for 25-30 minutes, or until done.

Serves 4-5

ITALIAN POT ROAST

4-5	pound beef chuck roast	1	4-ounce can mushrooms
1	tablespoon fat	1	8-ounce can tomato sauce
1	medium onion, diced	1	cup pitted ripe olives
1	teaspoon ginger		salt and pepper to taste

Brown onion in fat in heavy Dutch oven or skillet. When onion is transparent, move to one side of pan and brown roast, seasoning with ginger. Roast, covered, in 275 degree oven (very slow) about 2 hours. Add mushrooms, tomato sauce, olives, and salt and pepper. Continue to roast approximately 1 to 1½ hours, or until meat is very tender. Remove meat from the pot. To make gravy, skim off any excess fat from top of juices with spoon or baster. The remaining juices together with mushrooms, olives, etc., may be as thick as desired. If thickening is needed, make a paste of flour or arrowroot and cold water and add until the desired consistency is reached.   Serves 6

SURPRISE PACKAGES

Individual servings of steak, round steak, cube steak, patty of ground beef, etc.
1   teaspoon of onion soup mix per serving
     potatoes
     any desired vegetable, such as carrots, celery, green beans, etc.

Tear off a large square of aluminum foil for each serving. Center a serving of meat on each piece. Sprinkle onion soup mix over meat. Top with 1 peeled potato and any desired vegetable. Pull sides of foil up around food and seal tightly. Place on cookie sheet or in shallow pan and bake in 325 degree oven for one hour, or until meat is tender and vegetables cook to desired doneness. Very little cleanup with this meal!

TERIYAKI STEAK

1	flank steak	2	tablespoons brown sugar
1	teaspoon dry mustard	3	ounces soy sauce (this is about
1	teaspoon ground ginger		1/3 cup plus ½ tablespoon)

Score a flank steak lightly on both sides. Marinate in above mixture at least 3 hours, turning occasionally. Broil about 6-8 minutes on each side, or until done to your liking. The secret of a tender steak now remains in your slicing it as thinly as possible on a sharp diagonal slant. Serves 4

NOTE: If you should be spending the day on the road traveling, you can marinate the steak before leaving your campsite in the morning. Put one plastic bag inside another (being sure they are leakproof) and pour marinade into inner bag. Place steak in marinade and secure tightly with a twistie. Place bag in your kitchen sink. The motion of the trailer will marinate your steak beautifully. When you stop at the end of the day, it is a small matter to put a few coals on your portable barbecue; and your dinner is well on its way to being ready!

HAMBURGER POTATO CASSEROLE

A filling and good quick casserole.

1	pound ground beef	4	medium potatoes
	diced onion (or onion flakes)		salt and pepper to taste
1	can cream of chicken soup	½	soup can of milk

Brown ground beef with as much onion as desired. Then add chicken soup and cook a few minutes longer. Meanwhile, peel and slice the potatoes. Lay half of the potatoes in greased casserole. Pour over this the meat and soup mixture. Add remaining potatoes. Pour milk over all. Salt and pepper may be added as desired, though the soup does add salt to casserole. Cover and bake in 350 degree oven for 1 hour, or until potatoes are tender. Have a vegetable and a salad, and the dinner is ready! Serves 4

BASIC MEAT LOAF

2	pounds lean ground beef, chuck or round	1	tablespoon minced onion, or onion flakes
1	egg, slightly beaten		dash of pepper
2	teaspoons salt	½	teaspoon Accent
½	cup water or canned soup		your favorite herbs

Mix all ingredients together and pat into a greased loaf pan. If the meat is especially lean, lay 2 or 3 strips of bacon over top of meat loaf. Bake in 350 degree oven for 1 hour.   Serves 6

ALL-IN-ONE FAMILY DINNER

1	pound ground beef	1	can green beans (or 1 package frozen green beans)
1	small onion, sliced		
	salt and pepper to taste	½	teaspoon Worcestershire sauce
1	teaspoon Accent	1	pound can solid-pack tomatoes
4	medium potatoes, sliced ·		

Brown meat with onion, seasoning with salt, pepper, and Accent. Place potatoes in greased casserole; top with meat mixture. Next add can of green beans. Add Worcestershire sauce to tomatoes while still in can. (If the tomatoes are in very large pieces, run a sharp knife through contents of can a few times to break them up into smaller segments.) Pour tomatoes over meat, potatoes and beans. Bake in 350 degree oven for 1½ hours, or until potatoes are done.   Serves 4

STEAK BAKE

1	envelope mushroom soup mix	4	pounds chuck roast, cut 1½ inches thick
1	tablespoon minced onion		

Combine dry soup mix and onion flakes on a sheet of heavy foil. Roll roast in mixture until well coated. Then wrap loosely, sealing edges of foil. Place on cookie sheet or in shallow baking pan. Bake in 350 degree oven for 3 hours. Remove from oven. Open foil on top, being careful not to lose gravy. Place under broiler for 5 minutes, or until top is nicely browned. Slice into ¼-inch thick slices. Serve with gravy from package.   Serves 4-5

HEARTY SUPPER PIE

Prepare pie crust for a 2-crust pie, either from your own recipe, or a pie-crust mix. Line a large pie plate with one crust, reserving the other for the top.

1	pound ground beef	⅛	teaspoon allspice
½	cup milk	1	12-ounce package frozen hash-
½	package onion soup mix		brown potatoes (loose pack
	dash of pepper		type).

Combine meat, milk, soup mix, pepper and allspice. Put into pie shell, patting down lightly with back of spoon. Top with potatoes. Place top crust in position on pie, sealing edges and fluting. Cut several slits in crust. Bake in 350 degree oven 1 hour, or until well browned.   Serves 5-6

CRISPY BAKED CHICKEN

½	package Pepperidge Farm	1	cube butter, melted
	Stuffing		salt and pepper
1	chicken, cut in serving pieces		

Pour stuffing into a plastic bag and roll bag with rolling pin to make into fine crumbs. Dip chicken, a piece at a time, in butter and then roll it in crumbs until well coated. Place in shallow greased baking dish. Season with salt and pepper. Bake in 350 degree oven for 1¼ hours. (If you prefer, select only the pieces of chicken your family enjoys rather than the entire chicken.)   Serves 3-4

SIMPLE CHICKEN CASSEROLE

1	cup uncooked rice	1½	soup cans milk
1	can cream of mushroom soup	1	chicken cut into serving
½	package onion soup mix		pieces

Mix rice, mushroom soup, onion soup mix and milk together in a casserole. Lay pieces of chicken skin side down on top of rice mixture. Salt and pepper to taste. Bake in 250 degree oven for 3 hours, turning chicken once halfway through baking time.

Serves 4

HAWAIIAN CHICKEN

1½	cups pineapple juice	1½	teaspoons ginger
3	tablespoons soy sauce		dash of garlic salt
2	tablespoons salad oil	2	broilers
1	tablespoon sugar		

Combine juice and seasonings; bring to a boil in small saucepan. Salt and pepper broilers (or desired chicken parts) and broil for one hour, basting with marinade and turning pieces 4 or 5 times until chicken is tender and golden brown.   Serves 4-6

EASY CHICKEN CASSEROLE

1	can chicken with rice soup	1	cup boned chicken
1	can mushroom soup	½	cup diced celery
½	cup or 1 small can evaporated milk	1	4-ounce jar pimento, cut in strips
1	3-ounce can chow mein noodles	½	cup coarsely chopped nuts

Combine all ingredients in 2-quart casserole. Bake in 350 degree oven for 45 minutes to 1 hour.   Serves 4

FAVORITE HERB CHICKEN CASSEROLE

This is our favorite chicken casserole. It has a very distinctive taste and can be quickly prepared from pantry shelf ingredients.

1	can cream of chicken soup	⅛	teaspoon thyme
2	tablespoons minced onion	1 1/3	cups water
1	teaspoon salt	1 1/3	cups instant rice
	dash pepper	1½	cups boned, cooked chicken
½	teaspoon celery flakes	¼	teaspoon paprika
½	teaspoon parsley flakes		

Mix all ingredients except paprika together. Bake in covered casserole in 375 degree oven for 15-20 minutes. Remove cover and stir through the dish a few times. Replace cover and continue baking another 10 minutes. Sprinkle with paprika and serve.   Serves 4

BROILED HERB CHICKEN

2 tablespoons butter	¼ teaspoon basil
3 tablespoons lemon juice	salt and pepper to taste
¼ teaspoon thyme	1 chicken, cut in serving pieces

Melt butter and add seasonings. Brush some of this mixture over chicken pieces. Broil for 10 minutes (either in your oven or out of doors), turning chicken and brushing with butter mixture again. Continue turning and brushing occasionally for 40 minutes, or until chicken is tender and golden brown.   Serves 4

CHICKEN RICE BAKE

1 cup uncooked long grain rice	1½ soup cans milk
1 can cream of mushroom soup	½ package onion soup mix
	4 whole chicken legs
	parsley

In a low greased casserole, place rice. In small mixing bowl, combine mushroom soup, milk and onion soup mix. Pour this over rice, stirring to be sure rice is not sticking to the bottom of the casserole. On top of this place the chicken legs, skin side down. (Any combination of desired pieces could be used, of course.) Bake in 250 degree oven for 3 hours, uncovered, turning chicken over once to brown on skin side. Sprinkle chopped parsley or dried parsley flakes over casserole and serve. (This may be prepared ahead of time, covered, and stored in refrigerator until baking time.)   Serves 4

TURKEY (OR CHICKEN) DRESSING CASSEROLE

This is a different and delightful casserole making use of a prepared stuffing mix. It is a good way to use leftover turkey or chicken, but I find myself making it often with canned meat.

2 cups diced turkey	1 can cream of mushroom soup
1 4-ounce can mushrooms	1 can of cranberry sauce
1 package Pepperidge Farm Stuffing Mix	(whole berries)

Combine turkey (or chicken), mushrooms, and stuffing mix. Add mushroom soup and mix well. Bake uncovered in greased casserole in 350 degree oven for 20 minutes. Remove from oven and spread a can of cranberry sauce over top of casserole. Return to oven and bake another 10 minutes.   Serves 4-5

PREPARATION OF FISH

The preparation of most fish dishes is quick and easy. Outside of learning the basic steps of broiling, baking, etc., the one thing to remember is that fish should not be overcooked. Fish is basically tender to begin with. When broiling fillets, broil with the skin side down, and do not attempt to turn them over. When broiling a whole fish, this can be easily turned, as the skin and bone structure of the fish will hold it together.

FISH FOIL DINNER

For each person, place about a pound of whole fish on a good-sized sheet of aluminum foil. Place your choice of sliced vegetables and potatoes on top of fish. Season with salt and pepper and dot generously with butter. Bring sides of foil up around fish and seal securely. Bake in 400 degree oven for approximately one hour. This may also be baked on your charcoal grill. (My family especially enjoys Parmesan cheese sprinkled on the dinner as the packets are opened, or this may be added before baking if desired.)

BAKED MACARONI AND SALMON

1	cup cooked macaroni	1	teaspoon salt
1	cup canned salmon		dash of pepper
1	tablespoon melted butter	1	teaspoon chopped onion
1	tablespoon flour	1	teaspoon chopped green pepper
1	cup milk	¼	cup grated American cheese

Combine above ingredients and place in greased casserole dish. Stir together the following topping and sprinkle over casserole:

2   tablespoons melted butter   ¼   cup cracker crumbs

Bake in 350 degree oven for one hour.   Serves 4

CHOPSTICK TUNA

1	can cream of mushroom soup	1	cup chopped celery
¼	cup water	½	cup salted cashew nuts
1	3-ounce can chow mein noodles	¼	cup minced onion
1	7-ounce can tuna fish		dash of pepper

Combine soup and water, blending until all lumps have disappeared. Add remaining ingredients. Toss lightly. Place in low, flat casserole. Bake in 375 degree oven for 30 minutes.

Serves 4-5

TUNA BROCCOLI CASSEROLE

1	package frozen broccoli	½	soup can milk
1	7-ounce can of tuna, flaked	½	cup crushed potato chips
1	can cream of mushroom soup		

Heat oven to 450 degrees. Boil broccoli about 3 minutes and drain. Place in 1½ quart casserole. Cover with tuna. Mix soup and milk and pour over tuna. Sprinkle potato chips on top. Bake for 15 minutes.

Serves 4

SALMON MACARONI CASSEROLE

Combine the following ingredients in a greased casserole:

2	15-ounce cans macaroni in cheese sauce	¼	cup light cream
1	No. 1 can salmon, flaked	1	pimento, diced

Season to taste with salt and pepper. Sprinkle top with parsley and Parmesan cheese. Heat in 375 degree oven until it is bubbly and heated through.

Serves 4-6

SALMON LOAF

1	No. 1 can red salmon	¼	teaspoon pepper
2	tablespoons minced onion	½	teaspoon thyme
2	tablespoons minced parsley	1	cup cracker crumbs
2	tablespoons lemon juice	¼	cup milk (approx.)
½	teaspoon salt	2	eggs, well beaten
		2	tablespoons melted butter

Drain salmon, reserving the liquid in measuring cup. Flake salmon in mixing bowl. Add onion, parsley, lemon juice, seasonings, cracker crumbs. Toss lightly.

Add salmon liquid plus enough milk to make ½ cup. Add eggs and melted butter. Mix only until blended. Spoon into a greased 1 quart mold. Bake in 350 degree oven for 45 minutes.

Serves 4-5

(NOTE: A double recipe will fill a bread pan and makes a very good loaf for 8-10 persons).   Serve with shrimp sauce:

Heat a can of frozen shrimp soup, adding ¼ cup milk. Stir in a few sliced stuffed olives. Garnish serving plate with parsley and thin, curled lemon slices. (If you do not have a can of frozen shrimp soup available, make a thick white sauce, adding the stuffed olives).

CAULIFLOWER SHRIMP CASSEROLE

6	tablespoons butter	2	packages frozen cauliflower
4	tablespoons flour	2	pounds frozen shrimp (or canned)
2	cups milk	1	cup grated Cheddar Cheese
	salt and pepper to taste	1	cup slivered almonds

In saucepan melt butter. Remove from heat and stir in flour. Gradually add milk and salt and pepper. Stir over medium heat until thickened. In greased casserole dish place cauliflower sufficiently defrosted to separate the pieces. Top with shrimp. Pour cream sauce over this. Mix cheese and almonds and sprinkle over top. Bake in 350 degree oven for 40 minutes.   Serves 5-6

FIVE-CAN CASSEROLE

1	can tuna	1	can cream of chicken soup
1	8-ounce can milk	1	can chow mein noodles
1	can cream of mushroom soup		

Mix together all ingredients. (You may also add such things as cashew nuts, a bit of chopped celery, onion, etc.) Bake in greased casserole in 350 degree oven for 1 hour.   Serves 4-5

VERSATILE CASSEROLE

2 cups tuna, ham, chicken, or crab	1 teaspoon grated onion
1 cup diced celery	1 tablespoon lemon juice
1 cup cooked rice	3 hard-cooked eggs, sliced
¾ cup mayonnaise	½ teaspoon salt (omit if using ham)

Combine ingredients in greased casserole. Top with the following:

½ cup slivered almonds	1 cup crushed cornflakes

(Other toppings that can be used are crumbled bacon bits, French fried onion rings, etc.) Bake in 375 degree oven for 35 minutes.

Serves 4-5

SWEET-POTATO CASSEROLE

An excellent accompaniment to ham, this dish is prepared from canned goods and is a real favorite in our trailer.

1 No. 303 can apricot halves	1½ tablespoons butter
1 24-ounce can sweet potatoes	½ cup brown sugar

Drain apricots, reserving syrup. In greased casserole, place sliced sweet potatoes in alternating layers with apricot halves. Meanwhile, combine syrup from apricots with butter and brown sugar in a saucepan and boil rather rapidly until it becomes thick and syrupy (about 20 minutes). Pour syrup over casserole. Bake in 350 degree oven for 30 minutes, spooning syrup over ingredients occasionally so it is well glazed.

Serves 3-4

SWEDISH RICE PUDDING

This type rice pudding is served warm or cold with Swedish lingonberry sauce, a tart sauce like cranberries. It is a favorite Sunday evening buffet type dish in our home. I serve a jello mold, Swedish rye bread, pickled herring, Swedish meat balls, and various types of cheese with it.

1 cup rice	4 cups milk
3 eggs	cinnamon
½ cup sugar	butter
1 tablespoon lemon juice	

Using regular long-grain rice, cook according to directions. When not quite tender, drain water from the rice thoroughly. In large greased casserole, beat eggs slightly, add sugar and lemon juice. Gradually add milk. Spoon cooked rice into this mixture. Dot top with small pieces of butter and sprinkle with cinnamon. Bake in 350 degree oven for 1 hour, or until the rice seems completely set and no longer "wiggly" in center.   Serves 6-8

SIMPLE LASAGNE

8	ounces lasagne noodles	1	12-ounce carton small-curd
1	15½-ounce can spaghetti		cottage cheese
	sauce with meat	1	6-ounce package sliced
¼	teaspoon oregano		mozzarella cheese

Cook noodles in boiling water according to directions on package. Drain. Add the oregano to the can of spaghetti sauce. Using a 10x6 greased baking dish, make layers of the above ingredients in this order: half the noodles, half the cottage cheese, half the mozzarella cheese slices, and half the spaghetti sauce. Repeat with remaining amounts. Bake in 375 degree oven for 30 minutes.

Serves 4-5

CORNED BEEF WITH LIMA BEANS
(A quickie!)

2	packages frozen lima beans	¼	teaspoon salt
1	12-ounce can corned beef	⅛	teaspoon pepper
¼	cup diced onion	¾	cup milk
2	tablespoons butter	¾	teaspoon prepared mustard
2	tablespoons flour	1	8-ounce can tomato sauce

Cook lima beans in salted water as directed on package. (If you do not have frozen beans, substitute 2 cans lima beans. As you place them in dish, sprinkle with ½ teaspoon of salt.) Arrange beans in alternating layers with corned beef in greased baking dish. In small saucepan, melt butter, blend in flour, seasonings, and milk. Cook, stirring until thick. Blend together mustard and tomato sauce and pour over casserole. Bake in 350 degree oven for 30 minutes.   Serves 4

ARLENE SWANSON'S CASSEROLE

A recipe from my sister-in-law which through the years has been a real favorite:

1½	pounds pork sausage	2	packages chicken noodle soup mix
3	stalks celery, chopped	1	cup raw brown rice
1	medium onion, chopped	½	cup slivered almonds
1	green pepper, chopped (optional)	1	cup mushrooms
4½	cups boiling water		

Brown meat, celery, onion, and green pepper. Drain off all fat. Place in 2-quart greased casserole, add remaining ingredients, cover and bake in 350 degree oven for 1½ hours.   Serves 6

SAVORY CHIPPED BEEF CASSEROLE

1	12-ounce package medium-cut egg noodles	1	can cream of mushroom soup
		1	can whole kernel corn, drained
4	tablespoons butter	½	cup finely chopped green pepper
1	3-ounce jar chipped beef		buttered bread crumbs
4	tablespoons flour		

Cook noodles in salted water according to directions on package. Melt butter in skillet. Add chipped beef and cook until "frizzled." Add flour and blend in well. Add soup and cook, stirring constantly until sauce is smooth and thickened. Combine with corn, green pepper and noodles. Pour into greased casserole. Top with bread crumbs. Bake in 350 degree oven for 25 minutes, or until crumbs are browned and ingredients heated through.

Serves 4-5

TASTY SAUSAGE CASSEROLE

1	pound pork sausage (mildly seasoned)	½	cup finely chopped onion
		1	cup diced celery
1	cup raw rice	1	tablespoon soy sauce
1½	packages chicken noodle soup mix	2½	cups water
		½	cup slivered almonds

Break apart sausage and brown it in ungreased skillet. Pour

off any excess fat. Remove from stove. Add rice, soup, onion, celery, soy sauce, water, and almonds. Mix gently. Bake in 350 degree oven for 1 hour.

Serves 5-6

LUAU BARBECUED RIBS

4	pounds lean spareribs	1/3	cup ketchup
1	teaspoon salt	2	tablespoons soy sauce
	dash pepper	½	cup brown sugar
2	4½-ounce jars strained baby peaches	2	teaspoons ginger

Rub ribs on both sides with salt and pepper. Place ribs, meat side up, in foil-lined shallow pan. Bake in 450 degree oven for 15 minutes. Spoon off any fat from meat. While ribs are baking, prepare Luau sauce by combining the remaining ingredients in a small pan and bringing this to boiling point over medium heat. Pour sauce over ribs. Continue baking in 350 degree oven for 1½ hours, or until meat is tender, basting with sauce several times during baking period.

Serves 4-5

TASTY PORK ROAST

This roast may be prepared on a rotisserie in your oven, or over a barbecue spit out of doors. My sister Bonnie Opel prepared it at their lake home on a wooded shore in Northern Wisconsin, and it was the beginning of a treasured recipe for me.

5-6	pounds boneless, rolled pork loin roast	¼	cup peanut butter
		½	cup orange juice

Roast meat for approximately 3½ hours. Then mix together the peanut butter and orange juice, and use to baste the meat. Continue roasting and basting roast with the peanut butter-orange mixture for another 20 minutes or until you feel the roast is both well glazed and well done.

Serves 8

MARION SUNDSTROM'S VAGABOND PORK

2	pounds lean fresh pork shoulder, cut into ½ inch cubes	2	teaspoons salt
		1	teaspoon savory
		¼	teaspoon pepper
4	large onions, chopped	8	ounces noodles
2	cups chopped celery	¾	cup Cheddar cheese
2	1-pound cans tomatoes		additional ¾ cup Cheddar
1	4-ounce can mushrooms		

Brown meat slowly in a little fat in frying pan. While meat browns, combine onions, celery, tomatoes, mushrooms, salt, savory, and pepper in bowl. Grease your largest casserole and ladle about 1 cup of this mixture into dish. Cover with half of the noodles, half of the browned meat and ¾ cup grated cheese. Repeat layers of sauce, noodles and meat and top with sauce. Cover. Bake in 350 degree oven for 1½ hours. Uncover and sprinkle with additional Cheddar cheese. Bake 30 minutes longer, or until cheese is melted and top is golden brown.   Serves 12

NOTE: You may wish to make only half of this, as it is large, but you'll be surprised at how fast it goes — it's so very delicious!

GLAZED HAM LOAF

A delightful ham loaf with a tangy sauce. If you have any left over, it goes well into a sandwich, or can be reheated by wrapping in foil and heating in oven, or heated on top of the stove in the upper portion of your double boiler.

Have the butcher grind the following together for you:

2	pounds uncooked ground ham
1	pound uncooked ground pork

Other ingredients needed are:

1	tablespoon prepared mustard	1	teaspoon prepared mustard
		½	cup brown sugar
¾	cup milk	¼	cup cider vinegar
2	eggs	1	cup water
4	slices of bread, crumbled	¾	cup currant jelly
2	tablespoons cornstarch	½	cup raisins

Mix meat with the tablespoon of mustard, milk, eggs, and bread crumbs. Pack firmly into loaf pan. Then turn the loaf out onto lightly greased cake pan (or any pan slightly larger than loaf itself). Bake in 350 degree oven for 1 hour. While loaf bakes, prepare glaze. Combine cornstarch, mustard, and brown sugar. Stir in vinegar, water and currant jelly. Cook over medium heat until it is thick and bubbly. Stir in raisins. Spoon 1/3 of mixture over loaf at the end of the hour baking time. Return to oven for an additional 30 minutes. Serve the remainder of sauce, heated, with ham loaf.

Serves 8

SAUCY GREEN BEANS

2	packages frozen green beans	1	small can water chestnuts, drained and sliced
1	can mushroom soup		
½	cup milk	¼	teaspoon rosemary
¼	cup chopped onion	½	teaspoon salt
3	tablespoons chopped pimento	⅛	teaspoon pepper
		½	cup grated sharp cheese

Partially cook beans, leaving them just a bit crisp. Drain water from them. Combine all other ingredients except cheese in a 1½ quart casserole. Mix in the beans. Bake in 375 degree oven for 20 minutes. Sprinkle with grated cheese and bake 5 minutes longer, or until cheese has melted.

Serves 6

PEAS SUPREME

2	packages frozen peas	2	tablespoons pimento, diced
2	3-ounce cans mushrooms, drained		seasonings to taste (salt, pepper, etc.)
3	tablespoons butter		

Place all ingredients in a greased casserole. Cover and bake in 400 degree oven for 30 minutes, stirring after about 15 minutes to make sure ingredients are well blended.

Serves 6

BAKED CELERY

5	cups diced celery	1	can cream of celery soup
¾	cup grated cheddar cheese	1/3	cup slivered almonds
	dash of pepper	½	cup buttered bread crumbs
½	teaspoon paprika		

Place celery in a greased 9-inch shallow baking dish. Top with cheese and seasonings. Spoon undiluted soup over top. Sprinkle with almonds and crumbs. Bake in 350 degree oven for 45 minutes.   Serves 6

BEANS PARMIGIANA

1	package, each, of frozen	1	can cream of celery soup
	green beans		(diluted with ½ can milk)
	wax beans		salt and pepper
	lima beans	¼	cup grated Parmesan cheese

Cook beans according to directions on packages. Drain and mix with diluted soup, seasoning to taste with salt and pepper. Sprinkle grated cheese on top and bake uncovered in 350 degree oven until heated through, about 15-20 minutes.

NOTE: If I have pimento available, I add 2-3 tablespoons, minced, as its color adds eye-appeal.   Yield: 8-9 servings

OVEN-BROWNED POTATO FANS

Allow one medium potato per serving. Peel, lay flat lengthwise, and cut slices ¼-inch thick down through 2/3 of the potato. Put in shallow greased baking dish, spreading out the slices carefully the way you do butterflake rolls. Sprinkle with salt, pepper, and Lawry's seasoned salt. Pour melted butter over each potato. Bake in 400 degree oven for 45 minutes, or until done. Baste a few times during the baking period with the butter in the dish.

BUTTER BEANS

An ordinary can of butter beans is given a special flavor by the addition of 1/3 cup brown sugar and a few strips of bacon, diced and fried. Try it!

QUICK PARTY POTATOES

4-6   servings of instant
      mashed potatoes
	¼ cup grated cheese
	     salt and pepper

½ cup whipping cream	onion flakes

Prepare potatoes as directed on package. Place in greased casserole. Prepare topping by beating cream until whipped. Add grated cheese and season with salt, pepper, and onion flakes. Spread over potatoes. Place under broiler until cheese melts and it becomes golden brown, about 5-7 minutes.   Serves 4-6

SPINACH CASSEROLE

2 packages of frozen spinach	1 can cream of mushroom soup
3 tablespoons butter	½ cup dry bread crumbs
¼ cup diced celery	¼ cup butter
1 small onion, diced	

Cook and drain the spinach. In skillet, melt butter and cook celery and onion until transparent. Mix with spinach and mushroom soup. Pour into casserole. Brown bread crumbs in butter and sprinkle over top of casserole. Bake in 375 degree oven for 20 minutes.   Serves 4-5

WAYS TO CHANGE A LAYER CAKE MIX

To a white, yellow, chocolate, or lemon cake mix, add ½ cup finely chopped maraschino cherries and ½ cup chopped nuts. (Be sure the cherries are well drained before adding to cake batter.)

To a white, yellow, chocolate, or spice cake mix, add 2 tablespoons instant coffee. (This should be the finely ground instant coffee, not the freeze-dried variety.)

To any kind of chocolate or devil's food cake mix, add 2 teaspoons cinnamon, ½ teaspoon nutmeg, and ½ teaspoon ground cloves.

To any type mix except the spice, add 1 cup flaked, toasted coconut.

To any chocolate type mix, add ¼ teaspoon peppermint extract.

To a white cake mix, add ¼ teaspoon peppermint extract. Tint batter with green food coloring to desired shade.

If you do not wish to bake a layer cake in a large pan, following the directions on the cake mix box, use 2 tablespoons less water and bake in two greased and floured loaf pans, 9x5x3 for 35 to 40 minutes.

To bake an angel food cake mix in loaf pans, prepare batter as directed on box, and bake in two ungreased loaf pans, 9x5x3 for 40 to 45 minutes. Invert pans after removing from oven.

EASY MERINGUE CAKE

Follow directions for a yellow cake mix, except that for 2 eggs, use 4 egg yolks. Spread batter in 9x13 pan **and** an 8x8 pan. Beat 4 egg whites with ½ cup granulated sugar and ½ cup powdered sugar. Spread over batter. Sprinkle with slivered almonds. Bake in 325 degree oven for 40 minutes.

NOTE: In addition to serving it as it comes from the pan, this recipe makes a delicious torte when served with custard sauce, berries, or whipped cream.

DELUXE CAKES FROM MIXES

In this recipe you may use any cake mix or any flavor pudding mix you wish.

1	package cake mix	1	cup water (plus 2 tablespoons
1	package pudding mix		for chocolate chip and fudge
4	eggs		coconut mixes)

Combine all ingredients. Beat for 8 minutes at medium mixer speed.

Bake in 350 degree oven; time according to pan size:

2	9x5 loaf pans	45-50 minutes
1	9x12 pan	45-50 minutes
3	9-inch layer	25-30 minutes
1	10-inch tube	50 minutes

WACKY DEVIL'S FOOD CAKE

When I started experimenting with this cake, I was absolutely amazed at the moist, rich cake I could get using common staple foods carried in the trailer, and NOT EVEN A MIXING BOWL.

1½	cups flour	1	teaspoon vanilla
3	tablespoons cocoa	1	tablespoon vinegar
1	teaspoon salt	6	tablespoons cooking oil
1	cup sugar	1	cup water
1	teaspoon baking soda		

Sift the flour, cocoa, salt, sugar, and baking soda into an ungreased 9x9 or 10x8 pan. With a fork, stir around until ingredients are well blended. With the back of a spoon, form 3 holes in the mixture. Fill one hole with the vanilla, one with the vinegar, and the last with the cooking oil. Then pour water over all of it. With fork, mix thoroughly until all ingredients are well blended. (Batter will appear to be a bit lumpy.) Bake in 350 degree oven for 25 minutes, or until cake tests done with a cake tester or toothpick. Frost with favorite frosting or serve with whipped cream or ice cream.

NOTE: Almost the same results are obtained without bothering to sift dry ingredients first.

BARBARA STROM'S WESTHAVEN CAKE

1	teaspoon soda	1¾	cups flour
1	cup hot water	1	teaspoon cocoa
1	8-ounce package dates,	2	eggs
	finely cut	1	teaspoon vanilla
1	cup sugar	¼	cup chopped nuts
½	cup butter	¼	cup chocolate chips

Dissolve soda in hot water and pour mixture over dates. Set aside to cool. Cream together sugar and butter. Sift flour with the cocoa; then add eggs, vanilla, sugar mixture, dates; mix well. Pour into greased 9x13 pan. Sprinkle with nuts and chocolate chips. Bake in 350 oven for 40 minutes. If you wish to dress up your dessert, top with whipped cream or whipped topping. This cake keeps well and travels well.   10-12 servings

PINEAPPLE UPSIDE-DOWN CAKE

¼	cup butter	1	package yellow cake mix
½	cup brown sugar		maraschino cherries and pecan
1	8½-ounce can pineapple		halves (if desired)
	slices, drained		

Heat oven to 350 degrees. Melt butter over low heat in 8-inch square pan, 9-inch square pan, or a round layer pan. Sprinkle brown sugar evenly over butter. Arrange pineapple slices over sugar mixture. Place cherries and pecans in attractive design. Prepare cake mix as directed on package. Pour half of batter (about 2½ cups) over fruit in pan. Bake 35 to 45 minutes, or until tester comes clean. Invert immediately on serving plate. Leave pan over cake for a few minutes, then remove. The batter remaining may be baked in greased 8 or 9-inch layer pan as directed on package for a separate small cake.

For a larger cake: follow recipe above except use ½ cup butter, 1 cup brown sugar and 8-10 pineapple slices in oblong pan 13x9x2. Pour all of batter over fruit. Bake 45 to 55 minutes.

LEMON GINGERBREAD CAKE

¼	cup butter	1	package gingerbread mix
½	cup brown sugar		whipped cream
1	lemon		

Melt the butter in a 9-inch square pan. Blend in brown sugar until it is melted and smooth. Cut the lemon into very thin slices. Arrange slices evenly over the butter and sugar mixture. Prepare gingerbread mix according to directions on package. Pour batter over lemon slices. Bake at 350 degrees for 30 minutes. Invert pan over serving plate. Let remain on cake for a few minutes and then remove. Serve with whipped cream.

Yield: 9 servings

AUNT ROSE'S SOUR CREAM COFFEE CAKE

This recipe makes a delicious, moist cake that travels better than anything I know. It will keep for a week in your refrigerator, but your family will probably do away with it long before that.

¼	pound butter (1 stick)	1	teaspoon baking powder
1	cup sugar	1	teaspoon baking soda
2	eggs	2	cups flour
8	ounces sour cream	½	cup sugar
	pinch of salt	1	teaspoon cinnamon

Cream butter and sugar well. Then add eggs and beat until well blended. Add sour cream, salt, baking powder, baking soda and flour, beating until batter is smooth. In a small dish combine sugar and cinnamon. Place about one third of the batter in an ungreased angel food or bundt pan. Sprinkle with about a third of the sugar cinnamon mix. Add another third of batter to pan, repeating process with cinnamon mix. Place last third portion of batter in pan and top with remaining sugar mixture. With spatula, swish lightly through top of cake so sugar becomes mixed with batter. Bake in 350 degree oven for 40 minutes. Allow to cool 15 minutes before removing from pan to cooling rack.

Yield: 10-12 slices

QUICK COFFEE CAKE

Prepare a yellow cake mix as directed on package. Bake in a
9x13 greased and floured pan. When 15 minutes of the baking
time has elapsed, open oven door and sprinkle quickly the following mixture over cake:

½   cup melted butter   ½   cup chopped nut meats
½   cup brown sugar

Continue baking until time is completed. Yield: 10-12 slices

JELLO CAKE

(A quick, convenient, and different cake)

Follow directions for any white cake mix as given on package,
mixing into batter 3 tablespoons of packaged jello (any flavor you
wish). Reserve the remainder of jello powder for frosting. Bake
cake as directed either in round layers or one large cake. When
cool frost with following frosting:

JELLO FROSTING

All but 3 tablespoons from   1   cup sugar
   1 package jello   ⅛   teaspoon cream of tartar
¼   cup egg white   ¼   cup of water

Mix above ingredients together in top of double boiler. With
pan over boiling water, beat until icing holds soft peaks (about 4
minutes with an electric beater, or longer if you are using a hand
beater). Remove and continue beating until peaks stiffen and it is
of spreading consistency.   Serves 8

COLD WATER CHOCOLATE CAKE

1½   cups brown sugar   1   egg
½   cup shortening (butter if ½   cup sour cream
   using commercial sour   1   teaspoon soda
   cream)   1   cup cold water
2   squares unsweetened   2   cups flour
   chocolate   1   teaspoon vanilla

Melt chocolate and set aside to cool. Cream butter and
brown sugar. Add remaining ingredients, beating together until

well blended. Pour into 2 greased layer pans. Bake in 350 degree
oven for 20-25 minutes.   Serves 8

CAKE ROLL

4	eggs, separated	¾	teaspoon baking powder
¾	cup sugar	¼	teaspoon salt
1	teaspoon vanilla	¼	cup cocoa (optional)
¾	cup cake flour, sifted		

Beat egg yolks until thick and creamy. Gradually add sugar.
Add vanilla and beat well.

Sift together flour and baking powder and gradually add to
egg yolk mixture, beating only until smooth. (If chocolate cake is
desired, sift cocoa in with flour.)

Beat egg whites and salt until stiff, but not dry. Fold into
first mixture.

Line a jelly roll pan (10x15) with heavy brown paper and
grease generously. Pour cake batter into pan and bake in 375
degree oven for 15 minutes. Immediately upon removal from
oven, invert onto a towel which has been sprinkled with powdered
sugar. Beginning at one small end of cake, roll towel and cake
together and allow to cool in rolled position. When cool, unroll,
remove towel, and fill cake with any desired filling. Roll again.
(This cake freezes well, depending upon filling used.)

FILLINGS:

This cake roll may be filled with any softened ice cream, or
a filling of sweetened whipped cream. Two of my favorite fillings
are given below:

STRAWBERRY: Fold 1 ten-ounce package of drained
frozen strawberries into whipped cream. Roll into cake. For a
topping, bring to a boil ½ cup strawberry jam and ¼ cup light
corn syrup. Brush on top of cake, and pass remainder as sauce.

PINEAPPLE: Fold 1 nine-ounce can drained crushed pineapple into whipped cream. For top of cake, glaze with ¼ cup
apricot jam and ¼ cup light corn syrup that has been brought to
a boil.   Serves 8

ORANGE CHIFFON CAKE

2¼	cups sifted flour	6	egg yolks, beaten
3	teaspoons baking powder	¾	cup water
1	teaspoon salt	2	tablespoons grated orange rind
1½	cups sugar	6	egg whites
½	cup salad oil	½	teaspoon cream of tartar

Measure sifted flour. Add baking powder, salt, and sugar and sift again into mixing bowl. Make a well in the center of these ingredients with a spoon and add the next four ingredients in the order given. Beat until smooth.

In another bowl, beat egg whites and cream of tartar until very stiff. Carefully fold into batter until just blended. Pour into an ungreased angel food pan. Bake in 350 degree oven for 1 hour and 10 minutes. To keep cake from sinking and to cool it, invert the pan so that the center fits over an empty soft drink bottle for at least an hour before removing the cake from the pan. Serve with warm orange sauce:

WARM ORANGE SAUCE

2½	tablespoons quick-cooking tapioca	1	tablespoon butter
		2	cups sectioned orange slices
½	cup sugar		(or mandarin orange slices)
	dash of salt		few drops yellow food coloring
1¼	cups water		

Combine tapioca, sugar, salt, and water. Cook and stir until boiling. Remove and cool 5 minutes. Stir in butter, orange slices and food coloring. Serve warm over cake. (I often serve the cake with a scoop of vanilla ice cream, and then the sauce over it all. Delicious!)   Serves 12-14

FAVORITE OATMEAL COOKIES

This is the absolute favorite in our family. It travels well, and is
never made in a single batch, always double!

1	cup sifted flour	½	cup granulated sugar
½	teaspoon soda	1	egg
½	teaspoon salt	2	tablespoons milk
1	teaspoon cinnamon	1½	cups oatmeal
¼	teaspoon nutmeg		(quick-cooking oats)
½	cup butter	1	cup raisins
½	cup brown sugar		

Sift together the flour, soda, salt, cinnamon, and nutmeg.
Cream together butter, brown and white sugars. Add egg and
milk. Then add the dry ingredients. When well combined, add
oatmeal and raisins. Drop by spoonfuls on greased cookie sheet.
Bake in 375 degree oven for 8-10 minutes.   Yield: 3½ dozen

SWEDISH CARDAMOM DATE DROPS

2	cups sifted flour	¼	cup margarine
½	teaspoon baking soda	1	cup brown sugar, firmly packed
½	teaspoon ground	2	eggs
	cardamom	1	tablespoon milk
⅛	teaspoon salt	1	8-ounce package dates, chopped
½	cup butter	1	cup chopped walnuts

Sift flour, soda, cardamom, and salt together. Cream butter,
margarine, and brown sugar. Add eggs and milk. Next add the
dry ingredients a third at a time, beating well after each addition.
Stir in dates and walnuts. Drop by spoonfuls on ungreased cookie
sheet. Bake in 350 degree oven for 15 minutes, or until golden
brown.   Yield: 3½ dozen

TOFFEE BARS

1	cup butter		Topping:
1	cup brown sugar	1	7-ounce package semi-sweet
1	egg yolk		chocolate chips
3	drops maple flavoring		ground nuts (any kind)
2	cups flour		

Cream butter and sugar. Add other ingredients. Beat until it loses its flaky quality and becomes sticky. Spread in ungreased jelly roll pan or large cookie sheet that has 3 sides. Bake in 350 degree oven until lightly browned (for about 20 minutes). Remove from oven and sprinkle with chocolate chips. Return to oven for 3-4 minutes until chocolate begins to melt. Remove from oven and quickly spread chocolate with knife or spatula. Sprinkle with ground nuts. When chocolate has begun to firm up, cut into squares.   Yield: 5 dozen

CONGO BARS

2¾	cups flour	3	eggs
2½	teaspoons baking powder	1	teaspoon vanilla
½	teaspoon salt	1	cup chopped nuts
2/3	cup butter	1	6-ounce package chocolate chips
1	package brown sugar		
	(2¼ cups)		

Sift together flour, baking powder, and salt. Melt butter. Stir in brown sugar. When well blended, allow to cool slightly. Then add eggs one at a time, beating well after each addition. Add vanilla. Blend in dry ingredients, nut meats, and chocolate chips. Pour into greased 10x15 pan. Bake in 350 degree oven for 35 minutes.   Yield: 48 bars

ONE-BOWL LEMON SPICE BARS

2	cups flour	¼	cup brown sugar
½	cup butter, softened	½	teaspoon cinnamon

Mix together the above ingredients until crumbly. Pat into a 9x13 lightly greased pan, and bake in 350 degree oven for 10 minutes. While this bakes, prepare next layer:

3	eggs	½	cup raisins
2	cups brown sugar	½	cup chopped walnuts
½	teaspoon salt	2	tablespoons lemon juice
1	cup shredded coconut	1	teaspoon grated lemon rind

Using same bowl used for first mixture, blend the above ingredients. When first layer is baked, pour this mixture over it and continue baking for approximately 25 minutes more, until top is lightly browned. Cut when cool.   Yield: 4-5 dozen bars

BANANA CHOCOLATE CHIP COOKIES

¾	cup shortening (¼ cup butter	1	teaspoon cinnamon
	and ½ cup margarine)	¼	teaspoon nutmeg
1	cup sugar	1¾	cups quick-cooking oats
1	egg	1	cup mashed banana (about
1½	cups flour		2 medium)
½	teaspoon soda	½	cup chocolate chips
1	teaspoon salt		

Cream shortening and sugar. Add egg. Then add remaining ingredients. Drop by teaspoonfuls on ungreased cookie sheet. Bake in 375 degree oven for 12-14 minutes, or until lightly browned.   Yield: 8 dozen

CHOCOLATE CHIP BANANA BARS

2	cups flour	1	teaspoon vanilla
2	teaspoons baking powder	1	egg
½	teaspoon salt	1	cup mashed bananas (about
2/3	cup butter		2 medium)
2/3	cup granulated sugar	1	6-ounce package semi-sweet
2/3	cup brown sugar		chocolate chips

Combine flour, baking powder, and salt. Cream together shortening and sugars until well blended and fluffy. Beat in vanilla and egg. Blend in bananas and then the flour mixture. Stir in chocolate chips. Spread evenly in a greased 10x15 jelly roll pan. Bake in 350 degree oven for 20-25 minutes, or until golden brown. Cool for 15 minutes and then cut into bars.   Yield: 4 dozen

CREAM WAFER COOKIES

1 cup butter, softened	2 cups flour
1/3 cup cream	granulated sugar

Mix together the first three ingredients and chill for at least 1 hour. Then roll to ⅛-inch thickness. Cut in 1-inch rounds. (If you do not have a small round cutter, use edge of small glass or bottle top.) Spread sugar evenly over a piece of waxed paper. Transfer cookies to the paper and coat both sides with sugar before placing them on an ungreased cookie sheet. Prick each cookie about 4 times with a fork. Bake in 375 degree oven for 7-9 minutes. (Do not let them brown.) When the cookies are cool, put the following filling between each two.

Cream together well:

¾ cup sifted powdered sugar	1 teaspoon vanilla
¼ cup butter softened	few drops of food coloring
1 egg yolk	(optional)

Yield: 6-7 dozen

CONNIE TENGLIN'S FRUIT SPICE BARS

2 cups raisins	1¾ cups flour
1 cup sugar	1 teaspoon salt
1 cup water	½ teaspoon soda
¼ cup butter	1 cup chopped dates
1 teaspoon cinnamon	½ cup chopped walnuts
1 teaspoon nutmeg	½ cup chopped dried apricots (I
½ teaspoon ground cloves	cut mine with kitchen shears)

In saucepan combine raisins, sugar, water, butter, cinnamon, nutmeg, and cloves. Bring to a boil and boil for 3 minutes. Cool. Sift the flour, salt, and soda together. Add to first mixture when cooled to room temperature. Beat until well blended. Add dates, walnuts, and apricots. Spread in two 8x8 pans. Bake in 325 oven for 50-60 minutes.

Yield: 4-5 dozen

BEST EVER BROWNIES

This is an old family recipe for a very moist, cake-like brownie.

½	cup butter	2	eggs, beaten
2	squares unsweetened		pinch of salt
	chocolate	½	teaspoon baking powder
½	cup milk	1	teaspoon vanilla
1	cup sugar	¾	cup chopped nuts (optional)
2/3	cup flour		

In top of double boiler, melt together butter, chocolate, and milk. Set aside to cool. When room temperature, add remaining ingredients. Beat together well and pour into greased 9x13 pan. Bake in 350 degree oven for 25 minutes (or until it begins to pull away from edge of pan, and small holes appear in surface.) Frost with chocolate frosting when completely cool.   Yield: 4 dozen

CHOCOLATE CHIP BROWNIES

½	cup butter, softened	2	squares unsweetened chocolate,
1	cup sugar		melted
2	eggs	1	teaspoon vanilla
¼	teaspoon salt	½	package chocolate chips
½	cup flour		(3 ounces)

Cream together the butter and sugar. Add eggs. Then add remaining ingredients. Blend together well and pour into greased 9x9 pan. Bake in 350 degree oven for 20-25 minutes. Do not cut until completely cool.   Yield: 3 dozen

CHOCOLATE CHIP FRUIT BARS

1¼	cups flour	½	teaspoon almond extract
1½	teaspoons baking powder	1	6-ounce package chocolate chips
1	teaspoon salt	1	cup raisins
3	eggs	½	cup chopped maraschino cherries
1	cup sugar	1	cup chopped walnuts

Heat oven to 350 degrees. In a small bowl mix together flour, baking powder, and salt. In separate mixing bowl, beat eggs until light. Add sugar gradually. Add almond flavoring and dry ingredients. Fold in chocolate chips, raisins, cherries, and nuts. Bake in 9x13 pan for 30-35 minutes.   Yield: 4-5 dozen

BONNIE OPEL'S MILLION DOLLAR COOKIE

This is a recipe from my sister that makes a perfect sugar cookie. It is crisp and rich.

1	cup butter	2	teaspoons vanilla
1	cup margarine	4½	cups flour
1	cup white sugar	1	teaspoon baking soda
1	cup brown sugar	1	teaspoon salt
2	eggs	1	cup chopped walnuts (optional)

Cream shortening and sugars. Add eggs, vanilla, flour, soda, and salt. Shape into ¾-inch balls. Place on greased cookie sheet and flatten with bottom of small glass which has been dipped in granulated sugar. (I use one with a design on the bottom, thus transferring the design to the cookie.) Bake in 350 degree oven for 10 minutes, or until lightly browned.   Yield: 7-8 dozen

PUMPKIN SPICE COOKIES

1½	cups brown sugar	1	teaspoon cinnamon
½	cup butter (1 stick)	½	teaspoon cloves (ground)
2	eggs	½	teaspoon nutmeg
1¾	cups pumpkin	½	teaspoon salt
2¾	cups flour	1	cup chopped nuts
1	tablespoon baking powder	1	cup raisins

Cream sugar and butter. Add eggs one at a time, beating in well. Add pumpkin. In separate bowl, measure dry ingredients and stir them to mix. Add dry ingredients to pumpkin mixture. Stir in nuts and raisins. Drop by teaspoonfuls on ungreased cookie sheet. Bake in 350 degree oven for 12 minutes, or until lightly browned. Frost with following:

FROSTING

Mix together:

2½	tablespoons soft butter	1½	tablespoons milk or cream
1½	cups powdered sugar	¾	teaspoon vanilla

BUTTERSCOTCH BROWNIES

¼	cup butter	1	teaspoon baking powder
1	cup brown sugar (packed)	½	teaspoon salt
1	egg	½	teaspoon vanilla
¾	cup flour	½	cup chopped walnuts

Heat oven to 350 degrees. Melt butter in pan over low heat, being careful not to let it burn. Remove from heat and stir in sugar until it dissolves. Cool. Beat in egg, flour, baking powder, salt, and vanilla. Fold in nuts. Spread in greased 8x8 pan and bake 25 minutes. Cut bars while warm.

(NOTE: This recipe may be varied by substituting ½ cup of any of the following for the nuts: coconut, dates, pecans, raisins).

Yield: 3-4 dozen

BRAZIL BARS

This was given to me by Lorraine Peterson, who says: "Make 'em, then hide 'em, they're so good."

¾	cup butter	1	teaspoon vanilla
1	cup brown sugar	1	egg white
1	egg yolk	1½	cups slivered brazil nuts
1½	cups flour		

Cream butter and sugar. Add egg yolk, flour, and vanilla and mix well. Pat this mixture into a 9x9 pan. Brush dough with as much of unbeaten egg white as covers well. Sprinkle with brazil nuts. Bake in 375 degree oven for 15-20 minutes. Cut into squares and let cool in pan.

Yield: 20 squares

CHOCOLATE DATE BARS

This is a recipe for a nutlike chocolate date bar. It can be served warm with a scoop of vanilla ice cream, or can be cut into squares and enjoyed with a cup of coffee. It travels well!

	Filling:		Bottom and top layer:
2½	squares unsweetened chocolate	¾	cup softened butter
		1¼	cups brown sugar (firmly packed)
2/3	cup hot water		
1 1/3	cups sugar	1½	cups sifted flour
1 1/3	cups chopped dates	½	teaspoon salt
¼	cup butter	½	teaspoon soda
1	teaspoon vanilla	1½	cups quick cooking oats
		1	cup chopped walnuts

To prepare filling: In a small saucepan, melt chocolate with hot water. Over low heat, stir in sugar until dissolved. Add dates and cook, stirring, for about 5 minutes until it thickens. Remove from fire. Stir in butter and vanilla. Set aside while you prepare top and bottom crusts:

Cream together the butter and brown sugar. Stir in all the dry ingredients, oatmeal, and nuts. This will be a very crumbly mixture. Press half in bottom of a greased 9x13 pan. Spread the chocolate filling over it. Then sprinkle the remaining crust over the chocolate mixture. This is best done with one's hands. Bake in 350 degree oven for 30 minutes.   Yield: about 3 dozen

BUTTERSCOTCH TORTE

A quickly prepared torte which may be served with a topping of vanilla ice cream, or a dab of whipped cream.

1	package fluffy white frosting mix (for a 2-layer cake)	1	6-ounce package butterscotch chips
1	teaspoon vanilla	½	cup coconut
1	cup graham cracker crumbs	½	cup chopped pecans

Prepare frosting mix according to directions on package. Add the vanilla. Fold in all other ingredients carefully, and spread in greased 9-inch plate. Bake in 350 degree oven for 30 minutes, or until lightly browned.   Serves 8

WALNUT DELIGHT PIE

One of my absolute favorites. Because of the soda crackers, it is not too rich a dessert, but one on which you will receive many compliments.

3	egg whites	16	soda crackers (broken into
1	cup sugar		pieces size of cornflakes)
½	teaspoon baking powder		whipped cream
½	cup chopped walnuts		

Beat egg whites until stiff. Gradually add sugar and baking powder. With rubber scraper, gently fold in nuts and soda crackers. Spread in greased 9-inch pie plate. Bake in 350 degree oven for 30-40 minutes. Cool thoroughly, but do not refrigerate. First cut into wedges, then spread the entire top of pie with whipped cream.

NOTE: Grating a few curls of bitter chocolate over the top adds both to the taste and to the eye appeal.   Yield: 6 wedges

FRUIT COCKTAIL TORTE

This is a quick inexpensive torte which will be a welcome addition to any meal.

1	egg	1	No. 2½ can fruit cocktail,
1	cup flour		drained
1	cup sugar	½	cup brown sugar
1	teaspoon soda	½	cup chopped nuts
1/3	teaspoon salt	½	teaspoon cinnamon

Beat egg until fluffy. Then add flour, sugar, soda, and salt. Mix together well. Then add drained fruit cocktail, stirring until blended. Pour into 8x12 greased pan and spread evenly over bottom with spatula. Mix together the brown sugar, nuts, and cinnamon and sprinkle over batter. Bake in 300 degree oven for 1ʾhour and 20 minutes. Serve with whipped cream topping.   Serves 8-9

NORWEGIAN APPLE PIE

¾	cup sugar	½	teaspoon vanilla
½	cup flour	½	teaspoon salt
2	eggs	½	cup chopped nuts
1	teaspoon baking powder	1	cup peeled and diced apple

Combine sugar, flour, and eggs. Mix well and then add baking powder, salt, and vanilla. Stir in nuts and apple. Pour into 9-inch greased pie plate. Bake in 350 degree oven for 30 minutes. Cut in wedges when cool and serve with whipped cream or ice cream.   Serves 6

CHOCOLATE DATE PUDDING

1	8-ounce package dates, chopped	1 1/3	cups flour
		½	teaspoon salt
1½	cups boiling water	2½	teaspoons baking powder
1	teaspoon soda	½	cup chocolate chips
½	cup butter	½	cup chopped nuts
1	cup sugar	½	cup sugar
2	eggs		

Place dates in a small bowl. Mix soda into boiling water and pour over dates. In mixing bowl, cream butter and sugar. Add eggs one at a time, beating after each addition. Stir in date mixture. Combine flour, salt, and baking powder and add to butter mixture. Pour into greased 9x13 pan. Combine chocolate chips, nuts, and ½ cup sugar and sprinkle over top of cake. Bake in 350 degree oven for 35 minutes (or until a toothpick or cake tester comes out clean). Cut into squares and serve with ice cream or whipped cream.   Yield: 12-15 servings

NEVER FAIL PASTRY CRUST

A good recipe for the person who dreads pie making!

1	cup plus 2 tablespoons flour	1/3	cup oil
½	teaspoon salt	2	tablespoons cold water

Combine flour and salt. Blend in oil with a fork. Sprinkle water over mixture. Shape into ball. Flatten slightly and place between 2 sheets of waxed paper. Roll out to desired width.

Yield: 1 pie crust

NOTE: If baking one crust, place carefully in pie plate, turn under edge, form a fluted edge with your fingers, and then prick pie crust gently with a fork. Bake in 450 degree oven for 12 minutes or until lightly browned.

PRIZE PASTRY (2-crust)

2	cups flour	1	egg
1	teaspoon salt	1/3	cup water
2/3	cup shortening (Crisco)		

Sift flour and salt. Cut shortening into flour with pastry blender. Beat egg well and add water to it. Add the egg mixture to the flour mixture with blender and work until it begins to cling together and leaves the sides of the bowl. Divide in half and roll each portion out on floured board to the desired size. Proceed as above for bottom crust. Fit top crust over filling, and press edges of both crusts together. With a knife cut three or four slits in the top crust to allow steam to escape.

PECAN PIE

2	tablespoons flour	2	eggs
¾	cup sugar	½	cup evaporated milk
1	teaspoon salt	1	cup broken pecan pieces
1	cup Karo syrup (blue label)	¾	teaspoon vanilla

In a large bowl, mix flour, sugar, and salt. Add Karo syrup. With a fork, beat in eggs, one at a time. Add evaporated milk, pecans, and vanilla. Pour into 9-inch unbaked pastry shell. Bake in 375 degree oven for 50 minutes, or until center of pie is firm.

Serves 6

PERFECT CHEESE CAKE

¼	cup butter	½	cup sugar
1¼	cups graham cracker crumbs		pinch of salt
	(16 single crackers)	1	tablespoon lemon juice
1	8-ounce package cream	½	teaspoon vanilla
	cheese	2	eggs

Prepare a graham cracker crust by melting the butter and adding the graham cracker crumbs. Press into 9-inch pie plate. Set aside while filling is being prepared: Cream sugar and cream cheese (softened to room temperature) together. Add salt, lemon juice, and vanilla. Then add eggs one at a time, beating well after each addition. (With scraper, make sure the cream cheese is not sticking to sides of bowl.) Pour this mixture into graham cracker crust. Bake in 325 degree oven for 25-30 minutes.

Just before baking time is up, mix the following:

1	carton sour cream	½	teaspoon vanilla
2	tablespoons sugar		

Remove pie from oven and pour mixture of above ingredients over top of pie, spreading gently out to edges with knife or rubber scraper. Return to oven and bake 10 minutes longer. Remove from oven and cool before placing in refrigerator to chill. As this cheese cake freezes well, it is a good "make-ahead" dessert.

Serves 6-8

BEVERLY STROM'S CHERRY DESSERT

1	can cherry pie filling	2	sticks butter (½ pound)
1	package cake mix (spice		chopped nuts
	or yellow)		

Spread pie filling in bottom of greased 9x12 pan. Over this pour the cake mix in its powdered form. Shave 2 sticks of butter over cake mix and sprinkle with nuts. Bake in 350 degree oven for 45 minutes. This is an unbelievably simple and good dessert. Any desired pie filling or cake mix can be substituted for those above.

Serves 9-12

The following blank pages are for your own use.

V. LITTLE OR NO PREPARATION

HAM BALLS

1   3-ounce can deviled ham   crushed walnuts
1   3-ounce package cream cheese   parsley flakes

Mix ham and cream cheese. Shape into small balls and roll in crushed nuts and parsley flakes. Refrigerate until ready to serve. Serve on toothpicks.   Yield: about 2 dozen

PIZZA SQUARES

Bake 1 frozen pizza according to directions. When done, cut into bite-sized pieces. Serve warm.

CLAM DIP

1   8-ounce can minced clams,   ½   pint sour cream
    drained   ¼   pound cream cheese

Combine above ingredients. Season with onion juice, salt, and Worcestershire sauce to taste.   Serves 6-8

STUFFED CELERY

⅛   pound Roquefort cheese   dash of salt
¼   pound cream cheese   4   tablespoons mayonnaise
    juice of 1 small lemon   paprika
½   teaspoon Worcestershire sauce   celery cut in serving size pieces

Mash cheese with a fork. Blend in all other ingredients except paprika. Spread cheese mixture into curve of celery pieces. Sprinkle with paprika.   Yield: about 2 dozen

PICKLED ONION RINGS

These are excellent for deluxe hamburgers or tossed salad.

1	large sweet onion	1	6-inch stick cinnamon,
1	cup water		broken into pieces
1	cup white vinegar	2	teaspoons whole cloves
¼	cup sugar		few drops food coloring
½	teaspoon salt		

Thinly slice the onion and separate into rings (about 4 cups). Combine next 6 ingredients in saucepan. Cover and simmer 10 minutes. Strain. Add coloring. Pour hot mixture over onion rings. Chill at least 4 hours, turning over occasionally. Drain.

STUFFED EGGS

6	eggs, hard-cooked	1	tablespoon finely chopped
¾	teaspoon dry mustard		onion
½	teaspoon salt	1	tablespoon lemon juice
¼	teaspoon pepper	2-3	tablespoons mayonnaise or
¼	teaspoon Accent		sour cream

Cut hard-cooked eggs into halves lengthwise. Remove egg yolks carefully and place in small mixing bowl. Set the whites aside. Mash the egg yolks with a fork and stir in the remaining ingredients. When well blended, spoon mixture lightly into egg white halves, leaving tops mounded. Garnish center of eggs with a bit of pimento and parsley. Chill in refrigerator.

CHEESE DIP BALL

1	8-ounce package cream cheese	soy sauce
	minced onion to taste	parsley sprigs
	crushed pecans	

Soften cheese to room temperature. Blend in onion. Shape into ball, and roll in ground pecans. In mixing bowl approximately same size as ball, pour a little soy sauce. Place ball in soy sauce and marinate for several hours, turning occasionally so entire surface is marinated. Place on serving plate, garnish with parsley, and surround with crackers.

CHIPPED BEEF AND CREAM CHEESE BALLS

1   small jar chipped beef   1   3-ounce package cream cheese

Snip the chipped beef into very small pieces. Divide the cream cheese into 12 pieces and roll each piece into a ball. Toss balls in chipped beef until beef pieces adhere and ball is entirely covered. Put a toothpick in each ball and stick toothpicks into either a grapefruit or a large apple to serve.

BROILED GRAPEFRUIT

In center of carefully prepared grapefruit halves, sprinkle brown sugar. Add a dab of butter and brown lightly under low broiler heat. Remove when heated through and garnish with a maraschino cherry. Serve warm.

TOMATO BEVERAGE

1   8-ounce can tomato sauce
2   7-ounce bottles lemon-lime carbonated drink

Mix together in pitcher. Serve with ice cubes. Do not allow to stand in refrigerator or its fizziness will disappear.   Serves 4-5

INSTANT SPICED TEA MIX

A refreshing drink for either warm or cool weather, quickly prepared, and convenient to keep on your shelf.

2   cups Tang (powdered   ¾   cup Instant Tea (lemon flavored)
     orange drink)   1   teaspoon ground cloves
1   3-ounce package lemonade   1   teaspoon cinnamon
     mix (Wylers or Twist)

Mix together all ingredients until well blended. Add sugar to taste. Store in plastic container with tight-fitting lid. For iced tea: add 2 teaspoons of mixture per glass of cold water and serve with ice. For a cup of hot tea: pour boiling water over 1½-2 teaspoons of mixture.

SPICED CRANBERRY PUNCH

¼	teaspoon nutmeg	¾	cup sugar
¼	teaspoon cinnamon	1½	cups water
¼	teaspoon allspice	½	cup orange juice
3	tablespoons tea	¼	cup lemon juice
2½	cups boiling water	2	pints cranberry juice cocktail

Mix together nutmeg, cinnamon, allspice and tea in a cheese-cloth bag, or metal tea ball. Put into boiling water. Cover and let mixture steep about 5 minutes. Remove bag. Add sugar. Cover and cool. Add remaining ingredients, mixing well. Chill.

Yield: 2 quarts

CRANBERRY APPLE PUNCH

6	cups water	2	cups apple juice
1	cup sugar	1	cup black tea
1	quart cranberry juice cocktail	1	cup orange juice
1	5½-ounce can frozen lemonade concentrate		

Bring the water and sugar to a boil, stirring until sugar is dissolved. Add remaining ingredients. Chill before serving.

Serves 12-15

CHRISTMAS WASSAIL

4	lemons	1½	quarts water
4	oranges	1	cup sugar
2	sticks cinnamon	1	gallon cider
2	tablespoons allspice		

Cut lemons and oranges into quarters or eights, and simmer together with cinnamon, allspice, and water for about 1 hour. Pour through a strainer and add sugar and cider. Serve warm.

Serves 12-15

APPLE HONEY TEA

1	12-ounce can frozen apple cider	1	tablespoon honey
2	tablespoons instant tea	½	teaspoon ground cinnamon

In medium-sized saucepan reconstitute cider. Add remaining ingredients. Stir until well blended. Heat to serving temperature.   Yield: 1½ quarts

VIVIAN NORDEEN'S MOCHA NOG

1	quart eggnog	2	tablespoons coffee (powdered)
1	quart milk	1	quart vanilla ice cream
½	can Hershey's chocolate syrup		

Combine all ingredients, adding vanilla ice cream by spooning it into mixture in small pieces.   Serves: 8-10

LEMON ROLLS

3	tablespoons butter, softened	1	teaspoon grated lemon rind
1	teaspoon lemon juice	6	baked butterflake rolls

Combine butter, lemon juice, and lemon rind. Pull apart sections of rolls. Spread mixture into each section. Wrap rolls in foil and heat in 400 degree oven about 10 minutes, or until heated through.

NOTE: These lemon rolls are a delightful accompaniment to a summer fruit salad.

CAN-OPENER CHICKEN DINNER

(or "There never was a quicker dinner!")

1	No. 1 can green beans, drained	2	cans boned chicken (10 ounces)
1	can cream of mushroom soup	1	can chow mein noodles

Heat the beans, soup, and chicken together in a saucepan. Serve over chow mein noodles.   Serves 4

EASY SEAFOOD SUPPER

1	10-ounce can frozen cream of shrimp soup	1	tablespoon chopped parsley
½	cup light cream (or milk)	1	teaspoon lemon juice
2	cups shrimp		steamed rice or toast

Heat soup and cream or milk together slowly, stirring occasionally. Add shrimp, parsley, and lemon juice. Heat to serving temperature, but do not allow to boil. Spoon over steamed rice or buttered toast.   Serves 3-4

CHILI (QUICK AND EASY)

1	pound ground beef	1	can red kidney beans
1	bunch celery, sliced		salt and pepper to taste
1	onion, minced		chili powder to taste
1	can tomato soup		

Saute the ground beef, celery, and onion together for 10-15 minutes. Add remaining ingredients and simmer until good and hot.   Serves 4

RASPBERRY MOLD

1	3-ounce package raspberry jello	1	9-ounce can crushed pineapple, drained
1¼	cups hot water	1	large banana, cut in small pieces
1	12-ounce package frozen raspberries partially thawed	½	cup chopped nuts (optional)

Dissolve jello in hot water. Add raspberries and stir gently until separated. Chill until the consistency of egg white. Add pineapple and banana. Chill in mold. Serve with following sour cream dressing:

SOUR CREAM DRESSING

1	cup sour cream	1	tablespoon sugar
1½	cups miniature marshmallows	3	tablespoons lemon juice

Gradually stir marshmallows into sour cream. Add sugar and lemon juice, blending well. Store in covered container in refrigerator overnight before using.   Serves 5-6

MOLDED APRICOT SALAD

This is especially nice to serve in the fall because of the color of the apricots and prunes.

1	envelope Knox gelatin	1	banana, sliced
3	tablespoons lemon juice	1	cup cooked prunes, pitted and halved
1	12-ounce can of apricot nectar		
3	tablespoons sugar		

Soften gelatin in lemon juice. Heat apricot nectar and sugar until almost boiling point. Remove from stove and add gelatin, stirring until completely dissolved. Cool until slightly thickened. Add banana and prunes. Chill until firm.

Makes 1 small mold, or 7 individual molds

MOLDED FRUIT SALAD

1	package lemon jello	½	cup chopped walnuts
1	cup hot water	½	cup cut maraschino cherries
½	cup cottage cheese	1	cup crushed pineapple, drained
1	cup whipping cream		

Dissolve jello in hot water. Chill until partially set. Fold in remaining ingredients. Pour into ice cube tray and chill in refrigerator until set. Serves 8

LIME APPLESAUCE SALAD

1	No. 1 can applesauce	1	7-ounce bottle lemon-lime
1	package lime jello		carbonated beverage

Combine applesauce and gelatin in saucepan. Cook and stir until gelatin dissolves. Stir in lemon-lime beverage. Chill until firm. Serves 5-6

FALL SOUFFLE SALAD

1	package lime jello	½	teaspoon salt
1	cup hot water	1	cup unpeeled diced apples
½	cup cold water	¾	cup seeded red grapes
½	cup mayonnaise	¼	cup chopped walnuts
2	tablespoons lemon juice		

Dissolve jello in hot water. Add cold water, mayonnaise, lemon juice, and salt. Blend with eggbeater. Pour into refrigerator tray. Quick-chill for 15 minutes. Turn into bowl and beat until fluffy. Fold in apples, grapes, and nuts. Chill in mold.

Yield: 1 small mold

ORANGE DELIGHT SALAD

1	package orange jello	2	slices pineapple, diced
1	cup hot water	1	3-ounce package cream cheese,
1	cup frozen orange juice		cut in small pieces
24	miniature marshmallows	1	can mandarin oranges, drained

Dissolve jello in hot water. Add orange juice and chill until it reaches syrupy stage. Add remaining ingredients. Pour into mold and chill. Serves 5-6

MOLDED GRAPEFRUIT SALAD

2	envelopes unflavored gelatin	¼	cup sugar
½	cup cold water	1	No. 2 can grapefruit sections
¼	teaspoon salt	1	No. 2 can grapefruit juice

Soften gelatin in cold water in top of double boiler. Then place pan over boiling water and stir until gelatin dissolves. Add salt and sugar. Drain syrup from grapefruit sections and combine this liquid with the grapefruit juice to make 3 cups. Add this to gelatin, stirring until blended and dissolved. Fold in grapefruit sections and mold. Garnish with other fruits when serving.

Yield: 8-9 servings

LEILA WILSON'S BEAN SALAD

1	No. 303 can each:	1	green pepper, chopped
	french-style green beans	½	cup diced onion
	yellow wax beans		
	red kidney beans		
	Garbonzo beans		

Drain beans and marinate together with green pepper and onion in following mixture:

½	cup salad oil	½	cup sugar
½	cup vinegar		

Keep in refrigerator until ready to serve. An excellent buffet dish. Yield: 8-10 servings

SALMON MACARONI SALAD

2	cups cooked, cooled macaroni	1	teaspoon chopped parsley
		¾	cup mayonnaise
1	8-ounce can salmon, flaked	1	cup diced cucumber
1	teaspoon grated onion		salt and pepper to taste

Toss all ingredients lightly until blended. Chill.   Serves 4-6

PARTY SALAD

1 package lime jello	1 cup sour cream
1 package lemon jello	1 cup cottage cheese
2 cups hot water	1 cup sliced stuffed olives
1 No. 2 can crushed pineapple, drained	½ cup chopped walnuts

Dissolve jello in hot water. Add pineapple. Cool. Then stir in remaining ingredients. Pour into 2-quart mold. Chill until firm.

Serves 10-12

TUNA VEGETABLE SALAD

1 package lime jello	3 tablespoons vinegar
1 cup hot water	½ cup mayonnaise
½ cup cold water	salt and pepper to taste

Dissolve jello in hot water, then add the rest of the above ingredients. Beat with rotary beater or electric beater until frothy. When partially set, add the following ingredients:

1 can tuna, flaked	¼ cup grated cucumber
½ cup diced celery	2-3 green onions, sliced (use
1 cup shredded carrots	tops also)

Chill until firm in mold.

Serves 6

SWEDISH CUCUMBER SALAD

1 large cucumber	½ teaspoon salt
1/3 cup cider vinegar	few grains of white pepper
5 tablespoons water	1 tablespoon chopped parsley
5 tablespoons sugar	

Rinse and pare cucumber. Score the cucumber by pulling the tines of a fork lengthwise over it. Slice in very thin slices. Place in container that has a tight-fitting cover. Mix together the vinegar, water, sugar, salt and pepper and pour over cucumber slices, tossing lightly to coat evenly. Cover and chill in refrigerator for several hours to allow flavors to blend. When ready to serve, garnish with parsley.

Serves 3-4

FIVE CUP SALAD

1   cup orange sections   1   cup miniature marshmallows
1   cup pineapple tidbits   1   cup sour cream
1   cup coconut

Combine above ingredients and allow to stand for several hours before serving. Line bowl with cupped lettuce leaves and spoon salad into bowl.   Serves 6-7

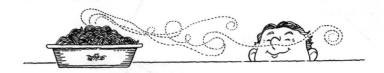

FRUIT SALAD DRESSING

This is quickly prepared and keeps well in the refrigerator.

1   egg   juice of 1 orange
1   cup sugar   juice of 1 lemon

In top of double boiler, beat egg well. Add sugar and blend well. Add juice of orange and lemon. Cook over boiling water until thickened. Serve over fruit salads and fruit jello molds.

CREAMY FRUIT DRESSING

¼   cup sour cream   1   tablespoon lime juice
2   tablespoons honey

Combine ingredients. Store in refrigerator.

TOMATO OIL DRESSING

1   can tomato soup   ¼   teaspoon pepper
¾   cup vinegar   1   teaspoon salt
¾   cup Wesson oil   ½   teaspoon dry mustard
¾   cup sugar   ½   teaspoon grated onion and its
1   teaspoon paprika   juice

Mix together well, either by beating with egg beater, or shaking in covered jar. Chill in refrigerator.

FRENCH DRESSING

¾	cup olive oil		salt and pepper to taste
¼	cup vinegar	1	peeled clove of garlic (optional)

Shake well before using.

COLE SLAW DRESSING

A delicious dressing for cole slaw is made by diluting mayonnaise with buttermilk to desired consistency. Season with salt and pepper to taste,

SIMPLE MAYONNAISE

1	teaspoon salt	2	tablespoons vinegar
¼	teaspoon paprika	2	cups salad oil
½	teaspoon dry mustard	½	cup lemon juice
2	egg yolks	1	tablespoon boiling water

Mix together the salt, paprika and mustard. Blend in egg yolks and vinegar. Add ½ cup of the salad oil, 1 tablespoon at a time, beating well with egg beater or electric beater. Add 1 more cup of the oil, a little at a time. Add the last ½ cup of oil alternately with the lemon juice. Beat in the boiling water. This recipe makes approximately 2 cups of fluffy mayonnaise. Variations can be made as follows:

SOUR CREAM MAYONNAISE: To ¼ cup of mayonnaise, add ¼ cup sour cream, dash of pepper, and chives.

FRUIT SALAD MAYONNAISE: To ½ cup of mayonnaise, add ¼ cup whipped cream.

PINK FRUIT DRESSING: To 1 cup of mayonnaise, add 1/3 cup cranberry juice cocktail.

THOUSAND ISLAND DRESSING: To ½ cup mayonnaise add 1 tablespoon chili sauce, a few chopped stuffed olives, ¼ teaspoon paprika, 1 hard-cooked egg, chopped, and salt and pepper to taste.

POPPY SEED MAYONNAISE: To ½ cup mayonnaise, add 1 tablespoon each of sugar, lemon juice, and poppy seed.

BROILED CRABMEAT BUNS

3	hamburger buns, split	¼	cup mayonnaise
1	6-ounce can crabmeat	½	cup diced celery
1	teaspoon Worcestershire sauce	6	slices American cheese

Butter all 6 bun halves. Mix the remaining ingredients, except cheese. Spread on the 6 halves, and top with cheese slices. Broil about 6 inches from heat until cheese melts and crabmeat mixture is heated through.   Yield: 6 servings

CHICKEN SALAD SANDWICH FILLING

2	cups boned chicken	1	tablespoon chopped pimento
½	cup slivered almonds		dash salt and pepper
½	cup finely chopped celery		

Mix ingredients with enough mayonnaise to moisten.

Yield: 6 servings

TUNA, SHRIMP, LOBSTER OR CRAB FILLING

1	can of any of the above fish	½	cup finely chopped celery
2	hard-cooked eggs, mashed	10	stuffed olives, chopped
1	teaspoon lemon juice		

Mix ingredients with enough mayonnaise to moisten and hold filling together.   Yield: 6 servings

CREAM CHEESE FILLING

1	3-ounce package cream cheese	½	cup chopped walnuts
	milk or cream		stuffed olives, chopped

Soften cream cheese with milk or cream to a good spreading consistency. Stir in nuts and olives. Blend well.

Yield: 3-4 servings

EGG SALAD SANDWICH FILLING

3	eggs, hard cooked and mashed	dash of onion salt
3	tablespoons finely chopped green pepper	½ cup chopped celery
	dash of salt	½ teaspoon prepared mustard

Mix ingredients with enough mayonnaise to moisten and be of spreading consistency. Yield: 6 servings

OPEN-FACE BACON AND TOMATO SANDWICHES

6	slices of bread (or English muffin halves)	oregano leaves
6	slices American cheese thin slices of tomato	12 slices of bacon

Partially fry bacon strips in skillet and remove to paper toweling to drain off any excess fat. Toast bread on one side under broiler. (Omit this step if using English Muffins.) Remove from broiler and butter untoasted side. Lay a piece of cheese on each slice of bread. Arrange thin slices of tomato on cheese and sprinkle with oregano leaves. Lay 2 strips of bacon on each sandwich. Return to broiler, and broil until cheese has melted and become bubbly. (Do not let bacon become too crisp or it will burn.) Serves 6

BROILER EGG CHEESE SANDWICHES

½	pound American cheese, shredded	2 hard-cooked eggs, chopped
2	teaspoons finely chopped onion	½ teaspoon Worcestershire sauce
1/3	cup chopped sweet pickle	¼ teaspoon salt
		½ cup mayonnaise

Mix all ingredients. Spread on hamburger or hot-dog bun halves. Place under broiler flame until cheese is melted and sandwich is slightly browned. (Do not place too near broiler heat or they will burn on top and not be heated through.)

Yield: 8 servings

"SLOPPY LOUIES"

(Your teenagers will love these!)

1 pound ground beef	1 tablespoon ketchup
1 can chicken gumbo soup	onion salt to taste
1 tablespoon prepared mustard	

Brown ground beef. Add remaining ingredients and simmer over low heat for 30 minutes. Serve in hamburger buns.

Yield: 4 servings

"NIBBLE MIX"

½ cup margarine	1 package each:
½ cup butter	thin pretzels
1 tablespoon Worcestershire sauce	Wheat Chex
celery salt to taste	Rice Chex
onion salt to taste	Cheerios
garlic salt (optional)	

Mix together the margarine, butter, Worcestershire sauce, and seasonings in low flat pan. Place in 250 degree oven for a few minutes to allow butter and margarine to melt. Stir until blended. Add cereals and leave in 250 degree oven for 1 hour, stirring occasionally so cereal is all coated. Serve as snack food.

BITTERSWEET CHOCOLATE TORTE

An unbelievably simple torte that can serve as "party fare." I have kept it for a week in my trailer refrigerator, so it is a dessert that can be prepared many days in advance of the time you wish to serve it.

1 frozen pound cake (such as Sarah Lee, etc.)	1 teaspoon instant coffee (powdered)
	1 cup sour cream
1 6-ounce package chocolate chips	

In top of double boiler, mix chocolate and instant coffee, stirring until chocolate is thoroughly melted. Remove from burner, add sour cream, a spoonful or two at a time, until entire amount has been added. (This insures a smooth texture.)

Cut cake into 7 thin layers. Place bottom layer on serving plate. (A few strips of waxed paper placed under cake, and removed when you are through frosting it, will insure a clean plate.) Spread chocolate over layer, adding another layer and frosting, until all 7 layers are stacked. Frost entire outside of cake. Store in refrigerator. (You might wish to add a few maraschino cherries on top of cake for decoration.)   Serves 6-8

PEACHY ORANGE SAUCE

1 package frozen peaches, slightly thawed	⅛ teaspoon cinnamon
	⅛ teaspoon salt
½ 6-ounce can frozen orange juice concentrate	

Combine all ingredients in saucepan. Bring to boil, lower heat, and simmer for 15 minutes. Cool slightly before spooning over vanilla ice cream.   Yield: 6 servings

LIME APPLESAUCE FLUFF

2 cups applesauce	2 bottles (small size) "7 Up"
2 packages lime jello	

Heat applesauce in saucepan and dissolve jello in it. Add the "7 Up". Pour into mold and chill. Serve with whipped cream.
                    Serves 6-8

"BUSY-DAY" LEMON CHEESECAKE

1 8-ounce package cream 1 package Jello lemon instant
   cheese   pudding mix
2 cups milk 1 8-inch graham-cracker crust

Allow cream cheese to reach room temperature. Soften cream cheese, blending in ½ cup milk. Add remaining milk and the pudding mix. With a rotary beater, beat just until well mixed (about 1 minute). Pour into graham-cracker crust. Sprinkle a few graham-cracker crumbs over top. Chill for at least 1 hour before serving.   Serves 8

BERRIES WITH CUSTARD SAUCE

Prepare one package instant vanilla pudding mix according to directions on package, but use only 2½ cups milk. Stir in ½ teaspoon vanilla. Chill. Spoon over fresh blueberries, raspberries, or strawberries.

STROM FUDGE SAUCE

3 squares chocolate ¼ teaspoon salt
½ cup water 4½ tablespoons butter
¾ cup sugar ¾ teaspoon vanilla

In a small saucepan bring chocolate and water to boiling point, stirring constantly until chocolate is melted. Add sugar and salt. Cook, stirring constantly until sugar is dissolved and mixture begins to thicken, about 5 minutes. Remove from heat. Stir in butter and vanilla. Cool. Makes 1½ cups fudge sauce for ice cream. Keep in covered container in refrigerator.

APRICOT COCONUT BALLS

1½ cups (6 ounces) dried 2/3 cup Eagle Brand sweetened
   apricots, ground, or   condensed milk
   chopped fine   confectioners sugar
2 cups coconut

In mixing bowl, blend together apricots and coconut. Stir in milk. Shape into balls. Roll in confectioners sugar. Let stand until firm.   Yield: about 6 dozen

SPECIAL K CEREAL BARS

½ cup sugar	4 cups Special K cereal
½ cup light corn syrup	3 1-ounce milk chocolate bars
1 teaspoon vanilla	1 cup butterscotch chips
¾ cup peanut butter	

Cook sugar and syrup until it reaches the boiling stage. Remove from heat. Stir in vanilla and peanut butter. Mix well. Add cereal. Press into buttered 9x9 pan. Cool. Melt chocolate bars and butterscotch chips and spread over bars. Cut into squares.   Yield: 1½-2 dozen

UNBAKED CHOCOLATE COOKIES

2 cups sugar	1 cup coconut
½ cup butter	1 teaspoon vanilla
½ cup milk	3 cups quick cooking oats
6 tablespoons cocoa	⅛ teaspoon salt

Combine sugar, butter and milk in saucepan and bring to a boil, stirring constantly. Then add remaining ingredients. Stir until mixed. Drop by teaspoonfuls onto waxed paper. Chill until set.   Yield: 3 dozen

FUDGE

A recipe for a fudge that will not turn sugary and keeps indefinitely.

1 cup evaporated milk	4-5 ounces unsweetened chocolate
4 cups sugar	1 pint marshmallow creme
21 ounces sweet chocolate (semi-sweet may be substituted if you prefer)	1½ cups chopped nuts

Cook milk and sugar for 5 minutes. Break chocolate into small pieces in large bowl and pour hot milk mixture over it. Beat until smooth. Stir in marshmallow creme and nuts. Pour into greased pan. Cool, store in refrigerator.

JIFFY FUDGE

(The quickest fudge imaginable!)

2 **tablespoons butter**	1 **box chocolate fudge frosting mix**
3 **tablespoons water**	

In top of double boiler, melt butter and add water. Blend in frosting mix. Over rapidly boiling water, cook for 5 minutes, stirring occasionally. Pour into greased loaf pan, 9x5x3, and let chill until firm.

Many variations of this can be made:

Add ½ cup chopped nuts to basic recipe.

Add 1 cup miniature marshmallows to basic recipe.

Add 2 cups raisins, or 2 cups pecans to basic recipe, and drop from teaspoon onto waxed paper. Chill clusters until firm.

TING-A-LINGS

2   **packages semisweet chocolate chips (12 ounces)**

4   **cups Cheerios or Kix cereal**

Melt chocolate in top of double boiler. Cool until room temperature. Fold in cereal gently, stirring only until well coated with chocolate. Drop teaspoonfuls onto waxed paper. Cool in refrigerator until chocolate is firm.   Yield: 3½-4 dozen

BUTTER CREAM FROSTING

2 **tablespoons butter**	1 **teaspoon vanilla**
1 **egg white**	½ **teaspoon almond extract**
2 **cups powdered sugar**	

Cream butter and unbeaten egg whites and beat thoroughly. Gradually work in sugar and flavorings. If a softer frosting is desired, add 1 tablespoon boiling water and beat well. To frost a 2-layer cake, make 1½ times this recipe.

LAZY DAISY CAKE TOPPING

(Sometimes referred to as a hot-milk topping)

1	cup brown sugar	1	3½-ounce packaged coconut
5	tablespoons cream	4	tablespoons butter (½ stick)
1	teaspoon vanilla		

Melt together the above ingredients. When cake has finished baking, take from oven and immediately spread with this topping. Place under broiler until it reaches desired brown shade.

LEMON CREAM BUTTER ICING

2	cups sifted confectioners sugar		grated rind of 1 lemon
2	tablespoons lemon juice	½	stick of butter (4 tablespoons), softened

Blend together the sugar, lemon juice, and lemon rind. Add the softened butter and stir it in thoroughly. When the mixture is velvety smooth, spread it over top and sides of cake.

CHOCOLATE WHIPPED CREAM

Below are two recipes for chocolate whipped cream. These may be used to frost an angel food cake that you have either bought or baked. Or you may slice the angel food cake, place a piece on serving plate, and put a spoonful or two of this whipped cream topping on it.

RECIPE I —

2	cups whipping cream	½	cup cocoa
1	cup powdered sugar		dash salt

Mix thoroughly and chill in refrigerator for at least an hour. Beat until it reaches spreading consistency.

RECIPE II —

1	cup whipping cream	4	tablespoons cocoa
½	cup granulated sugar		

Mix thoroughly and chill in refrigerator for at least an hour. Beat until it reaches spreading consistency.

PINEAPPLE NUTMEG SAUCE

¼ cup sugar	1 cup crushed pineapple,
1 tablespoon cornstarch	undrained
dash of salt	1 tablespoon lemon juice
¼ teaspoon ground nutmeg	1 teaspoon vanilla

Combine sugar, cornstarch, salt, and nutmeg in a small saucepan. Add pineapple and lemon juice and mix well. Stir and cook over medium heat until boiling point is reached. Remove from heat and add vanilla. Cool. Chill and serve over vanilla ice cream.

Serves 6

QUICK AND EASY CARAMEL SAUCE

1 package dry caramel frosting	3 tablespoons soft butter
mix	2/3 cup milk
2 tablespoons light corn syrup	

Combine frosting mix, corn syrup, and butter in top of double boiler. Gradually stir in milk. Heat over boiling water for 5 minutes, stirring occasionally. Serve warm over ice cream, cake, or pudding. To store: keep in covered container in refrigerator.

NOTE: A good chocolate sauce may be made by substituting 1 package dry chocolate fudge frosting mix for the caramel mix.

BUTTERSCOTCH SAUCE FOR WAFFLES OR PANCAKES

1¼ cups brown sugar	4 tablespoons butter
2/3 cup corn syrup	¼ cup heavy cream

Blend these ingredients and bring to a boil, stirring constantly. Simmer 20 minutes over low heat, stirring occasionally. Serve warm over waffles or pancakes.

ORANGE BASTING SAUCE

An excellent sauce for your ham or lamb.

1	10-ounce jar currant jelly	¼	teaspoon pepper
¼	cup orange juice	1	teaspoon salt
1	teaspoon grated orange rind	1	tablespoon prepared mustard

In a small saucepan, combine all ingredients and simmer for about 5 minutes, stirring constantly. Use sauce to baste your ham or lamb during its last 30 minutes of roasting.

CHERRY SAUCE FOR HAM

An interesting change from the traditional raisin sauce served with ham.

1	can sour red pitted pie cherries	2	tablespoons cornstarch
		¼	teaspoon cinnamon
¾	cup sugar	½	lemon, thinly sliced

Drain juice from cherries, reserving it as base for sauce. In a saucepan combine sugar, cornstarch, and cinnamon. Add the cherry liquid, and cook until thickened, stirring constantly. Add cherries and lemon. Simmer for 15 minutes. Remove lemon and discard. Serve warm over ham.

TART RAISIN SAUCE FOR HAM

¼	cup brown sugar	3	tablespoons lemon juice
1	tablespoon flour	½	cup raisins
1	cup water	1	tablespoon butter
¼	teaspoon salt	¼	cup chopped walnuts

Mix sugar and flour and gradually add water. Cook, bringing to a boil and stirring constantly. Add salt, lemon juice, and raisins and simmer 5 minutes. Remove from heat. Add butter and walnuts and stir until butter is melted. Serve warm over ham.

SPEEDY SAUCE

For a thrifty, speedy sauce, heat a can of celery, chicken, Cheddar cheese, tomato, or cream of vegetable soup with enough milk to give the desired consistency.

EASY BARBECUE SAUCE

1	can tomato soup	1	tablespoon brown sugar
¼	cup sweet pickle relish	1	tablespoon vinegar
¼	cup diced onion	1	tablespoon Worcestershire sauce

Combine all ingredients. Cover and simmer until onion is cooked and all flavors have blended. Yield: 1½ cups

BASIC WHITE SAUCE

For 1½ cups thin white sauce:

1	tablespoon butter	¼	teaspoon salt
1	tablespoon flour	1½	cups milk
	white pepper		

For 1 cup medium white sauce:

2	tablespoons butter	¼	teaspoon salt
2	tablespoons flour	1	cup milk
	white pepper		

For 1 cup thick white sauce:

3	tablespoons butter	¼	teaspoon salt
4	tablespoons flour	1	cup milk
	white pepper		

Melt butter in saucepan over low heat. Blend in flour, salt, and dash of white pepper. Add milk, stirring until well blended. Cook, stirring constantly till mixture thickens and bubbles.

The following blank pages are for your own use.

APPENDIX

TABLE OF MEASUREMENTS

3	teaspoons	1	tablespoon
2	tablespoons liquid	1	ounce
6	tablespoons	⅜	cup
4	tablespoons	¼	cup
5 1/3	tablespoons	1/3	cup
8	tablespoons	½	cup
16	tablespoons	1	cup
1	cup	8	ounces or ½ pint
2	cups	1	pint
4	cups	1	quart
2	pints	1	quart
4	quarts	1	gallon
8	quarts	1	peck
4	pecks	1	bushel
2	tablespoons fat or butter	1	ounce
	butter size of an egg	2	ounces or 4 tablespoons
1	stick butter	½	cup
1	pound granulated sugar	2	cups
1	pound brown sugar	3	cups (not packed)
1	pound confectioners sugar	3½	cups
1	pound flour	4	cups
1	pound rice	2	cups
1	pound pitted dates	2	cups
1	square chocolate	1	ounce
16	large marshmallows	¼	pound
1	pound cranberries	4	cups
1	pound ground beef	2	cups
1	cup whole eggs	5	eggs
1	cup lemon juice	4-6	lemons
1	pound shredded coconut	5	cups

MEASUREMENTS AND EQUIVALENTS

Many people are puzzled when a recipe calls for a certain amount of a specific food. Below is a table of common foods, showing how quantities can be converted.

Apples, fresh	1 pound - 3 medium apples or 3 cups sliced
Apricots, dried	1 pound - 3 cups uncooked, 5 cups cooked
Asparagus	1 pound - 16 to 20 stalks
Bacon	6 lean pieces - 1/3 cup crumbled
Bacon	3 lean pieces - 3 tablespoons crumbled
Bacon, lean uncooked	1 pound - 24 slices
Bananas	1 pound - 3 medium bananas
	1 pound - 2½ cups sliced
	1 pound - 2 cups mashed
Beans, white	1 pound - 2½ cups
Berries	1 quart - 2½ cups
Berries, strawberries	1 pint - 1½ to 2 cups hulled
Bread crumbs dry	1 pound - 2 cups
Bread crumbs dry	1 slice bread - 1/3 cup crumbs
Bread crumbs, soft cubes	1 pound, 1 ounce loaf - 11½ cups (with crust)
Bread crumbs, dry cubes	1 slice dry bread - ¾ cup crumbs
Bread cubes, soft	1 slice fresh untrimmed bread - 1 cup
Bread stuffing prepared	8- ounce bag - 3 cups (one package makes enough for a 5-pound chicken, 2 bags enough for a 10-pound turkey)
Brussel sprouts	1 pound - 1 quart or less
Cabbage	1 pound - 4 cups shredded
Candied peels, mixed	1 pound - 2½ cups chopped
Carrots	1 pound - 5 medium or 2½ cups diced
Cheese, American	1 pound - 4 to 5 cups grated
Cheese, Cheddar	1 pound - 4 cups grated
Cheese, Cottage	½ pound - 1 cup
Cheese, Cream	3 ounces - 3 tablespoons

Cheese, Cream	8 ounces - 1 cup
Chicken	1 pound dressed - 1½ cups boned
Chicken, boned	3 cups - 5 cups ground
Chicken, breast	1 large - 1 cup boned
Chocolate, unsweetened	1 ounce - 1 square or ¼ cup grated
Citron	4 ounces - ½ cup
Coconut, flaked	3½-ounce package - 1 1/3 cups
Coconut, shredded	4-ounce package - 1½ cups
Coffee	1 pound - 80 tablespoons
Corn flakes	18-ounce package - 16 to 20 cups
Cornmeal	1 pound - 3 cups uncooked, 4 cups cooked
Crackers, graham	9 coarsely crumbled - 1 cup
Crackers, graham	12 finely crushed - 1 cup fine crumbs
Crackers, soda	22 finely crushed - 1 cup fine crumbs
Cranberries	1 pound - 4 cups sauce
Cream, heavy	½ pint - 2 cups whipped
Cream, sour	½ pint - 1 cup
Currants	11-ounce package - 2 cups
Dates, pitted	8-ounce package - 1 cup whole or 1¼ cup cut up
Egg whites	1 cup - 8 to 12
Egg yolks	1 cup - 12 to 14
Eggs, whole large	1 cup - 5
Flour, all purpose	1 pound - 4¾ cups sifted
Flour, cake	1 pound - 3 to 4½ cups sifted
Flour, cake	1 cup - 1 cup plus 2 tablespoons all purpose flour
Flour, rye	1 pound - 5 cups sifted
Flour, whole wheat or graham	1 pound - 3½ cups sifted
Fruit peels, candied	4-ounce container - ½ cup
Gelatin, unflavored	1 envelope - 1 ounce
Lemon	1 medium - 3 tablespoons juice
Lemon rind	1 medium - 1 teaspoon grated rind
Macaroni	1¼ to 1½ cups - 2¼ cups cooked

Marshmallows	¼ pound - 16 marshmallows, large
Marshmallows, miniature	10 - 1 large marshmallow
Meat, ground raw	1 pound - 2 cups
Milk, evaporated	14½-ounce can - 1 2/3 cups
Milk, evaporated	6-ounce can - ¾ cup
Milk, sweetened condensed	15-ounce can - 1 1/3 cups 14-ounce can - 1¼ cups
Mushrooms	1 pound - 35 to 45 medium sized with stems
Noodles	1½ to 2 cups - 2¼ cups cooked
Nuts in shell: Almonds	1 pound - 2 cups nut meats
Peanuts	1 pound - 2 cups nut meats
Pecans	1 pound - 2 cups nut meats
Walnuts	1 pound - 2 cups nut meats
Nuts, shelled: Almonds	1 cup - 4 ounces
Peanuts	1½ cups - 7 ounces
Pecans	1 cup - 3 ounces
Walnuts	1 cup - 4 ounces
Onions	1 medium - ½ cup chopped
Onions	1 pound - 3 large
Peaches	1 pound - 4 medium or 2½ cups peeled and sliced
Peanut butter	8-ounce jar - 1 cup
Peas in pod	1 pound - 1 cup shelled
Pineapple	2 pounds - 1 medium
Plums	1 pound - 8 to 20 depending on variety
Potatoes, sweet	1 pound - 3 medium or 3 cups sliced
Potatoes, white	1 pound - 3 medium or 2½ cups sliced
Raisins	15-ounce package - 3 cups, not packed
Rhubarb	1 pound - 2 cups cut into ½ inch pieces 3 cups cut - 2 cups cooked
Rice, brown	1 cup - 4 cups cooked
Rice, long grain white	1 cup - 4 to 4½ cups cooked
Rice, precooked white	1 cup - 2 cups cooked
Rice, wild	1 cup - 4 cups cooked

Rolled oats, quick cooking	1 cup - 1¾ cups cooked
Shrimp: Small size	1 pound - 60 or more
Average size	1 pound - 26 to 30 in shell
Jumbo size	1 pound - 15 to 18 in shell
Cooked and cleaned	1 cup - ¾ pound raw or 7 ounces frozen shelled
Spaghetti	1 to 1¼ cups - 2¼ cups cooked
Sugar: Brown	1 pound - 2¼ cups firmly packed
Confectioners	1 pound - 4 cups sifted or 3½ cups unsifted
Granulated, white	1 pound - 2¼ cups
Granulated, brown	1 cup - 1 1/3 cups firmly packed
Superfine	1 pound - 2 1/3 cups
Tomatoes	1 pound - 4 small
Vanilla wafers	30 small, finely crushed - 1 cup fine crumbs
	20 small, coarsely crushed - 1 cup
	1 pound - 4 cups finely crushed

(Because you may be adding recipes for many dishes not included in this text, I have made the baking charts much more comprehensive than needed for this book alone.)

OVEN TEMPERATURES

Slow Oven	250 to 325 degrees F.
Moderate Oven	325 to 375 degrees F.
Moderately Hot Oven	375 to 400 degrees F.
Hot Oven	400 to 450 degrees F.
Very Hot Oven	450 to 500 degrees F.

BAKING CHART

	Minutes	Oven Temperature
YEAST BREADS		
Loaves	50 to 60	400 F.
Rolls	20 to 30	400 F.
QUICK BREADS		
Biscuits	12 to 15	450 F.
Corn bread	25 to 30	400 F.
Gingerbread	30 to 40	325 F.
Muffins	20 to 25	400 F.
Nut bread	50 to 60	350 F.
Popovers	30 to 40	425 F.
PASTRY		
Pastry shell	12 to 15	450 F.
2-Crust with cooked filling	25 to 35	425 F.
2-Crust with uncooked filling	30 to 45	400 F.
Custard type or pumpkin	35	400 F.
Meringue shell	10 to 15	350 F.
COOKIES		
Drop	10 to 15	400 F.
Rolled	8 to 12	400 F.
Refrigerator	8 to 12	400 F.
Pan	25 to 30	350 F.

CAKES

	Minutes	Oven Temperature
Angel	60	325 F.
Sponge	60	325 F.
Fruit	2 to 4 hours	250 F. to 275 F.

Cakes with shortening:

	Minutes	Oven Temperature
Cup cakes	20 to 25	350 F.
Layers	25 to 30	375 F.
Loaf	45 to 60	350 F.
Sheet	15 to 30	375 F.

MEATS:

	Minutes	Oven Temperature
Beef, rare	18 to 20 per lb.	300 F.
Beef, medium	22 to 25 per lb.	300 F.
Beef, well done	27 to 30 per lb.	300 F.
Lamb, pink	15 per lb.	325 F.
Lamb, well done	30 per lb.	300 F.
Pork	40 per lb.	350 F.
Ham, smoked	30 per lb.	300 F.
Veal	30 per lb.	325 F.
All rolled roasts	Add 10 to 15 per lb.	
Chicken	25 per lb.	350 F.
Duck	25 per lb.	325 F.
Turkey, small	25 per lb.	300 F.
Turkey, large	20 per lb.	325 F.
Fish	20 per lb.	375 F.

BROILING CHART

(Because steaks vary so in size, amount of bone, etc., this chart can only be approximate). Preheat broiler for 10 minutes, broil meat on one side using chart below. Season as you wish, turn and broil approximately same length of time on second side. You may check for desired doneness by slashing slightly near bone and noting color of meat.

Filet mignon, Delmonico, rib, club,
porterhouse, or small sirloin
    1 inch thick   5 minutes (rare)
                                  6 minutes (medium)
                                  7 to 8 minutes (well done)
    1½ inches thick   9 minutes (rare)
                                    10 minutes (medium)
                                  12 to 13 minutes (well done)
    2 inches thick   16 minutes (rare)
                                    18 minutes (medium)
                                  12 to 13 minutes (well done)

Large sirloin
    1 inch thick   7½ minutes (rare)
                                    9 minutes (medium)
                                    10-12 minutes (well done)
    1½ inches thick   10 minutes (rare)
                                    12 minutes (medium)
                                    14 minutes (well done)

Hamburgers
    ¾ inch thick   4 minutes (rare)
                                    6 minutes (medium)
                                    7 minutes (well done)

Lamb chops
    1 inch thick   6 minutes (medium)
                                    7 minutes (well done)
    1½ inches thick   9 minutes (medium)
                                    11 minutes (well done)

Cured ham slices
¾ inch thick	6 to 7 minutes (well done)
1 inch thick	9 to 10 minutes (well done)

NOTE: To broil frozen meat, use a low temperature so the surface does not char before the interior thaws and cooks. Allow 1½ to 2 times as long as specified in above chart.

CAN SIZES

Size	Weight	Cups
6-ounce	6 ounces	¾ cup
8-ounce	8 ounces	1 cup
No. 1 (picnic)	10½ ounces	1¼ cups
No. 300	15½ ounces	1¾ cups
No. 303	1 pound	2 cups
No. 2	1 pound, 4 ounces	2½ cups
No. 2½	1 pound, 13 ounces	3½ cups
46 ounces (No. 3 cylinder)	46 ounces	5¾ cups
No. 10	106 ounces	12 to 13 cups

SUBSTITUTIONS

If you don't have this:	You can use this:
1 tablespoon cornstarch	2 tablespoons flour
1 cup sifted all-purpose flour	1 cup plus 2 tablespoons sifted cake flour
1 cup sifted cake flour	1 cup minus 2 tablespoons sifted all-purpose flour
1 teaspoon baking powder	½ teaspoon cream of tartar with ½ teaspoon baking soda
1 cup sour milk	1 cup sweet milk with 1 tablespoon vinegar
1 square chocolate (1 ounce)	3 tablespoons cocoa with 1 tablespoon butter
2/3 cup honey	1 cup sugar in 1/3 cup water
1 whole egg	2 egg yolks and 1 tablespoon water
1 cup canned tomatoes	1 1/3 cup chopped fresh tomatoes simmered 10 minutes
½ cup catsup or chili sauce	½ cup tomato sauce with 2 tablespoons sugar, 1 tablespoon vinegar, and ⅛ teaspoon ground cloves
1 teaspoon Worcestershire sauce	1 teaspoon bottled steak sauce
½ cup tartar sauce	6 tablespoons mayonnaise with 2 tablespoons chopped pickle relish
1 cup tomato juice	½ cup tomato sauce with ½ cup water
1 cup canned beef bouillon	1 beef bouillon cube dissolved in 1 cup hot water

If you don't have this:	**You can use this:**
1 cup canned chicken broth	1 chicken bouillon cube dissolved in 1 cup hot water
½ pound mushrooms	1 4-ounce can mushroom caps
1 3-ounce can Chinese noodles	2 2½-ounce cans potato sticks
1 10-ounce package frozen strawberries	1 cup sliced fresh strawberries with 1/3 cup sugar
1 pound shrimp, shelled, deveined and cooked	1 5-ounce can shrimp
1½ cups diced cooked ham	1 12-ounce can pork luncheon meat, diced
1 teaspoon pumpkin pie spice	½ teaspoon cinnamon, ¼ teaspoon ginger, ⅛ teaspoon ground nutmeg, ⅛ teaspoon cloves

WAYS TO USE LEFTOVERS

In a day when food costs continue to rise, all of us realize the importance of economizing wherever it is possible. Don't throw away food that is leftover. Put your cooking skill and imagination to work and create tasty leftovers.

Some foods that are left make good second meals merely by reheating. Others can be prepared in a new way with sauces, crisp toppings, seasonings, etc. Here are some of the ways in which leftovers may be put to good use:

Use **BREAD** in:
Bread pudding
Croutons
Crumbs for breading fish,
    poultry, or meat

Use **SOUR CREAM** in:
Cookies, cakes
Beef Stroganoff
Salad dressings
Sauces for vegetables

Ways to Use Leftovers (continued)

Use BREAD in:
Fondues
French toast
Salmon loaf, Meat loaf

Use BUTTERMILK in:
Cookies, cakes
Quick breads

Use COOKED FISH,
POULTRY, MEATS in:
Casseroles
Creamed foods
Curries
Hash
Salads
Sandwiches

Use COOKED
VEGETABLES in:
Casseroles
Creamed dishes
Meat or poultry pies
Salads
Sauces
Scalloped dishes
Soups
Stews

Use COOKED OR
CANNED FRUITS in:
Fruit cups
Fruit sauces
Gelatin desserts
Quick breads
Salads
Shortcake
Upside-down cake
Yeast breads

Use EGG YOLKS in:
Baked custard
Cookies, cakes
Scrambled eggs

Use EGG WHITES in:
Cakes
Meringues

Use HARD-COOKED
EGGS in:
Casseroles
Egg sauce
Salads

Use COOKED
POTATOES in:
Fried or creamed potatoes
Meat or potato patties
Soups, chowders, stews
Salads

Use COOKED RICE,
NOODLES, SPAGHETTI,
MACARONI in:
Baked macaroni and cheese
Casseroles
Salads
Spanish Rice

Use COOKIES OR
UNFROSTED CAKE in:
Ice-cream sandwiches
Toasted cake slices, served
with fruit or ice cream

MASTER CHECK LIST

(You may want to add items of your own to this, or use the
additional space for check-off purposes.)

GENERAL ITEMS:

basic tools
bedding
  blankets
  pillows
  sheets and pillow cases
  sleeping bags (if preferred)
camera equipment
clothesline and pins
first-aid kit
flashlights, lanterns
fly swatter
games
kitchen towels and dishcloths
matches
needle and thread
outdoor barbecue
  barbecue utensils
    (long forks, etc.)
  charcoal
  charcoal lighter
paper products
  aluminum foil (both heavy
    and light weights)
  facial tissue
  paper napkins
  paper plates and cups
  paper toweling
  plastic bags
  toilet tissue
  wax paper
pencils and paper

Check List (continued)
personal items
   clothing
   drug items
   soiled clothing bag
   toilet articles
plastic pail
plastic outdoor tablecloth
rain wear
   boots
   rain coats
   umbrellas
small radio
soap (bar soap and liquid soap)
towels and washcloths
TV tables

KITCHEN ITEMS:
baking pan (8-inch square)
bottle opener
bread board
bread pans (2)
can opener
carving knife
cookie sheet (can double as tray)
cooking fork
cooking spoon
double boiler
dutch oven (Teflon lined) or
   large casserole
egg beater
hand electric beater (for
   occasions when you are
   hooked to electricity)
hot pad holders
kitchen tongs

Check List (continued)
measuring cups
measuring spoons
muffin tin
paring knife
pie plate
plastic containers with lids for
  storage
plastic dishes
plastic mixing bowls
plastic pitcher
potato peeler
rolling pin
rubber scraper
salt and pepper shakers
saucepans (2 or 3)
shallow roasting pan
sifter
skillet
soup ladle
spatula
stainless steel flatware
strainer
your copy of *Cooking on Wheels*

FOOD ITEMS:

spices and condiments:
baking powder
baking soda
chili powder
cinnamon
cloves
ginger
ketchup
minced garlic
minced onion flakes

mustard
nutmeg
paprika
parsley flakes
pepper
salt
soy sauce
vanilla extract
vinegar
Worcestershire sauce

suggested pantry foods:
cake and frosting mixes
cocoa
coffee
coffee cake mixes
cold drink mixes
crackers
dehydrated potatoes
dry cereals
dry soup mixes
dry yeast
flour
gelatin mixes
jams and jellies

mayonnaise
muffin mixes
oil or shortening
pancake mix
pancake syrup
peanut butter
pie crust mixes
pudding mixes
rice
spaghetti and noodles
sugar
tea

Because there are many CANNED GOODS that one might keep in the trailer, and families have different tastes and eating patterns, I hesitate to mention any, except to say that I usually try to carry some of the following with me:

Chinese noodles
chow mein
corned beef hash
a few cans of fruits

ham
spaghetti sauce
tuna, salmon, etc.
white potatoes

REFRIGERATOR AND FREEZER ITEMS:

Many of the items listed below will just be transferred from your home refrigerator to the trailer refrigerator when you leave home:

bacon	eggs
butter or margarine	lettuce
carrots	milk
celery	tomatoes
cheese	

INDEXES

(Editor's Note: In the belief that it will be more convenient for the reader, we have divided the index into two parts, one for general information and top of the stove cooking, and the other for dishes requiring oven cooking.)

GENERAL AND TOP OF STOVE COOKERY INDEX

USING YOUR OVEN